FRIENDS FOREVER?

"Linda said I was her best friend forever. And I said she was mine. Why couldn't we go to the same school?"

—Marion Coleman Brown

FAR FROM HOME

"I hate it here. We can't go in the lake, or ride the horses or anything. It's as bad as being in South Carolina. I thought it was different up north."

—Sarah Bracey

NO LIMITS

"Hundreds of thousands of my elders had negotiated, marched, sung, shouted, demanded, and died. Why couldn't I be president? If I played my cards right, a talented young fellow like me could even—go to Yale!"

—Ben Bates

Dreaming in Color, Living in Black and White

Our Own Stories of Growing Up Black in America

Dreaming in Color, Living in Black and White

OUR OWN STORIES OF GROWING UP BLACK IN AMERICA

Laurel Holliday

Abridged Young Readers Edition

SIMON PULSE
New York London Toronto Sydney Singapore

First Simon Pulse edition March 2003
Text copyright © 2000 by Laurel Holliday

This book is an abridged edition of the previously published work: *Children of the Dream: Our Own Stories of Growing Up Black in America* copyright © 1999 by Laurel Holliday

SIMON PULSE
An imprint of Simon & Schuster
Children's Publishing Division
1230 Avenue of the Americas
New York, NY 10020

Printed in USA

10 9 8 7 6 5 4

ISBN 0-671-04127-4

Contents

Introduction

———◆———

Now is the time to make justice a reality for all
of God's children. . . . I have a dream my four
little children will one day live in a nation where
they will not be judged by the color of their skin
but by the content of their character.
I have a dream today!

—DR. MARTIN LUTHER KING JR., "I Have a Dream,"
delivered at the March on Washington
for Civil Rights, August 28, 1963

In this anthology, African-Americans from across
the United States invite us into their childhoods.
Carrying on a long-standing black autobiographi-
cal tradition, the writers recount the struggles, as
well as the joys, of growing up in twentieth-
century America. In poignant, personally revealing, and often highly entertaining true stories,
they tell us what it was like to grow up stigma-
tized by the color of their skin, yet often very
proud of their heritage, their culture, and their
community.

In the context of the writers' own personal
experiences, we learn of the persistent racial
inequities that black youth have been faced with
over the course of the twentieth century. At a time

in their lives when they might simply need to focus on growing up, they are forced to deal with racism.

But the writers also write about their resilience and how they learned to transmute injustices into determination to achieve racial justice. As such, the writings here are a testament to the endurance of Dr. Martin Luther King Jr.'s dream, the courage of black youth, and the role of creativity in the redemption of racism.

Amitiyah Elayne Hyman

$\blacksquare\!\!\!\!-\!\!\!-\!\!\!\!\blacklozenge\!\!\!-\!\!\!-\!\!\!\!\blacksquare$

A minister in the Presbyterian church for eighteen years, Amitiyah Elayne Hyman began her own company called SpiritWorks in Washington, D.C., in 1998. Consulting with individuals and institutions, she designs prayers and rituals that assist people with self-acceptance, self-love, and the ability to be open and vulnerable to others. As a "mixed-blood woman," she brings African, Native American, and European traditions together in her rituals.

Amitiyah's writing also serves as a healing ritual. "Racism fed a cycle of abuse in which I was trapped as a child," she says, "and writing out this story helped me to heal from that abuse." In this true story she revisits the horror she felt in 1948, when she was first forced to defend herself against a racial epithet.

When I asked Amitiyah for her thoughts about Dr. Martin Luther King Jr.'s dream, she said that it is no longer applicable. "The twenty-first century will be the time for people of color, the earth's majority, to come into their own. King's dream is *too small* for the future."

STICKS AND STONES
AND WORDS AND BONES

We only met outside, in air that was cold and stung our faces, or in warm breezes that invited us to catch lightning bugs before bedtime. We cherished these sidewalk encounters, escapes from overheated kitchens and sun-starved hallways, an older sister's bossiness, and forced afternoon naps. They made us feel special, adventurous, beyond the limits imposed on kindergartners in a steel-workers' town on the Ohio River in 1948.

We would sit on the steps of the house between our two houses—a buffer zone that held our little end of the block, of blue collars and rednecks and black professionals, together. Swaddled in maroon corduroy leggings or knee-padded overalls, blue wool peacoats, rubber boots, and mismatched mittens that never wanted to stay on our hands, we enjoyed each other.

Passersby might have guessed that we were the best of friends, or cousins perhaps, from the way we whispered and laughed into each other's faces in the middle of winter. They would have

missed that our faces were the colors of sweet
vanilla and caramel cream, that my thick dark
braids were rebelliously unraveling in the moist
heat of my scalp, and that her short, straight
blond hair was stringy and wet in the dampness.
Our heads were hidden, sweating inside earmuffs
and knitted caps, which taunting boys, from
across the street, dusted white with well-aimed
snowballs.

Our shovels, wooden sleds, and buckets lay
nearby. Once we began to talk, they seemed to
fall away, forgotten in the rush of intimacy. We
discarded imaginary playmates, birthday gifts,
and Christmas favorites as if they had been
leaky boots or outgrown sweaters. Somehow we
understood that as long as we stayed in the safe
zone between our two houses and came when
mothers clapped or called, we could continue
the giggling and tickling and the whispering
games we'd grown to love. We played patty-
cake and hopscotch back and forth, first on one
leg, then on the other, in foot-high mounds of
snow.

> Little Sally Walker, sitting in a saucer,
> Wipe your weeping eyes.
> Rise, Sally, rise.

At first we didn't notice that our mothers kept
their distance. They never ventured out of
shaded doorways or warm kitchens to chat or to
see what was going on. They didn't join in

our laughter and whispering. Instead, they vigilantly kept themselves apart, watching for us through screened doors and upstairs bedroom windows. We made an unspoken pact with them—if they allowed us to cross yards and fences, then no one else need go beyond the boundaries or break invisible barriers set up by city sidewalks, conforming siblings, and disapproving fathers. Our little-girl forays compensated for grown-up dislikes and distances, for long held habits of fear.

She first said the words, after we marveled about the storm the night before and the way the moon said "hush" over the blanketed street. They fell out of her lips like jacks from her hand, plopping haphazardly onto the brick-and-concrete steps that had been shoveled earlier in the day. The sting of them sent tremors through my body that found a resting place in the soft tissues of my heart. They froze the spot and sent chills down my arms. They numbed my fingers.

"NIGGER. My daddy says that you're a NIGGER."

"Never let anyone call you NIGGER," was the mantra my father had drilled into my head.

Hot tears swirled up from somewhere deep, spilled out onto flushed cheeks, dripped into my lap. They warmed my hands and released my stiff fingers. I began to shake uncontrollably as I reached for a piece of brick, lying near the stoop, to steady myself. I snatched off my mittens. My fingers tore at the stone. Curling themselves around it, they locked onto its sharp, frozen hardness.

Sticks and stones can break my bones
but words can never harm me . . .
Sticks and stones can break bones and words . . .
Break bones and words can . . .
Harm me . . .

She saw the impact her words had upon my body as they flew from her thin lips, forming tiny darts of puffy gray-white air. They seemed to hang suspended in the stinging cold for an instant before they pierced my flesh. Then they disappeared into the frost. As if to prolong their power, she fired them rapidly, over and over again:

NIGGER, NIGGER, NIGGER, NIGGER,
Nigger,niggerniggerniggerniggernigger
niggerniggerniggernigger . . .

It was the way we played; we repeated grown-up words, trying them on for size the same way we donned dress-up clothes and pretended we were adults. If one word was sufficient, then we'd say ten for rhythm's sake. They tickled our mouths. It was fun, we thought, repeating grown-up words.

But I couldn't laugh with her. This word had hit its mark. I was impaled on it. In the background, I heard the drone of numerous warnings, the veiled threat of my gruff-voiced father. From that moment on, I believed that something terrible was going to happen to me. I knew I had set an unalterable chain of events into motion. I feared that they would avalanche, burying me in shame. I was cursed, doomed. I had let somebody call me "NIGGER." It wasn't just any old body, either; it was my friend. That really hurt.

Before I could stop myself, I wrenched out the loosened brick, heavy in my little girl's unmittened hand, and lifted it to her head, smashing it into her face. I heard the crack as it connected with her forehead in a well-positioned strike. The boys across the street howled and hooted their approval. She screamed in pain. Blood began to spread over her eyebrows, dripping into her eyes, rolling off her nose, down her snotty lips, and over her trembling chin. It pooled, making large polka dots on her play clothes.

For a moment we were freeze-framed by the clash of energies. Her words and my well-aimed brick had done what wary mothers could not do. The safe zone between our houses melted like snow, evaporating in the scorch of this ancient battle, begun by great-grandparents centuries ago. Now we played out the script. We ran to our mothers, scrambling in terror, falling in and out of snowdrifts. Skidding over the porch, I leapt into the vestibule, scattering icy wetness everywhere. I hurled myself through the doorway into the outstretched arms of my mother. She'd heard the wailing and had seen me coming from the lace-curtained living room window.

My father, who had been working in his second-floor study, raced downstairs to us. I was sobbing, and I didn't want to tell him what had happened. I was fearful of his wrath; after all, hadn't I let someone call me "NIGGER"? I had survived her teasing, but could I stand up to his hot anger? Too many tongue-lashings and belt strappings told me that was impossible.

My heart was hammering. I could have exploded. My chest wall, brains, and clenched teeth wanted to shatter like icicles into sharp pointy pieces. My father tried to wrench me loose from my mother. I tried to avoid his grip. Gasping for air, I twisted toward my mother and buried my face in her aproned belly.

The glass door of the house began to shake. My father whirled around in response to the pounding and the pacing on our porch. I saw her father's red menacing face. His shirttails flew from unbuttoned pants that he hadn't bothered to cover with a jacket. The two men glared at one another, straining shoulders, flexing arms, rocking back and forth on their heels. My father wore his slippers; her father had on metal-clipped boots. My mother peeled me loose from around her waist and took up a position at my father's side. Together they formed a phalanx, an impenetrable wall against him. Her father yelled and paced, threatening me and my parents.

Standing tall with stone-still faces, they held

their ground. They refused him access to me. My father snarled as he spit words out: "I've told Elayne never to let anyone call her NIGGER. She was obeying my instructions."

What he didn't say in that moment was that he himself had called me "little nigger" more times than I care to remember. It was a mean "pet" phrase, handed down from one generation of colored to another. It migrated, in their mouths, from the deep south of Edisto Island, South Carolina, to Pittsburgh, Pennsylvania. It took up residence in his mouth. He used the phrase like a stick, stalking me and my older sister. Whenever we displeased him, he struck us with it. I felt helpless in those moments, unable to defend myself, knowing that I could not go up against this big man's insults with my little girl's body, my little girl's hate, my little girl's hurt.

All of those "little niggers" coalesced around the big one I'd heard just moments before. Together they formed a tight fist, knotting beneath the surface of my skin. The knot remains. That brick-bearing little girl stays with me. She is vigilant and available, should the need arise, to explode against taunts and bullies. Now she has a well-stocked arsenal and seldom wears mittens.

Our friendship ended on a day when brooding clouds swirled past steel mills, sullied snow drifted into puddles and onto porches. Our intimacy terminated with her father's insolent retreat from our porch. She traveled through icy streets, past snowbound buildings, to the hospital where doctors stitched her face. I cried, watching the empty street from my bedroom window. Cold wind stirred cruel words and frigid rage into a witches' brew of sticks and stones. Together they erased the spot where we had laughed and whispered, before the blood ran down.

Marion Coleman Brown

Now in her forties and working as a counseling psychologist, home-based publisher, and writer, Marion Coleman Brown has devoted much of her life to helping the handicapped. "I look ahead and plow paths for those who have given up on life," she says, "people who are hurting, sick, neglected, abused, misunderstood, depressed." Particularly important for her is helping children to realize their full potential. "I am an encourager, a planter, a waterer," she says, "and I believe in children first, always."

In this very moving story of her relationship with her first playmate and friend, "blond-haired, blue-eyed Linda," Marion shows how internalized self-hatred, passed on from one generation of blacks to another, can be just as destructive to children as white prejudice and bigotry.

"Because of my childhood experiences, I am who I am today," Marion says. "But it took me forty years to get here, to a life of self-love and self-respect."

MY FIRST FRIEND
(MY BLOND-HAIRED, BLUE-EYED LINDA)

Who was your first playmate? Do you remember? And who was your first friend? Were they one and the same? It doesn't often happen that way. But to me it did. I remember mine—I can't help but remember her. She was blond-haired, blue-eyed Linda. I had never seen a white girl up close before, and she had never seen a black girl up close before. Getting to be with her was like being with the Queen of England. So it seemed, at least by my grandmother's standards.

I belonged to my grandmother during the summer months, to have and to hold for better or for worse. Everybody called her by her nickname, Big Mama. I often wondered why such a name was given to such a scrawny little woman. I guess part of it was how she could have her way with you. When you heard that raspy voice, you'd think thunder and lightning were about to strike you dead. She was always towering over me like she was some cousin of the mighty King Kong, assessing my every move and emotion.

I never could understand how quiet and hum-

11

ble she became when Linda and her parents came
up the hill to see her. I had never seen my grandmother that way before—so submissive, and
every sentence she uttered ending with, "Yes,
ma'am, Miss Thelma," "Yes, sir, Mr. Ancil," and
"Yes, ma'am, Miss Linda." "Miss Linda!" I said to
myself, almost choking from what I'd heard. Why
in the world was Big Mama calling her Miss Linda
and answering her with "Yes, ma'am"? Linda was
as young as I was—no more than six or seven
years old. For the life of me, I couldn't understand
what Big Mama was doing.

She was scaring me to death. Where was the
woman I knew? Vanished without a trace. I've
seen dried-up prunes with more spirit!

"Ugh, ugh," I said. These people must be something awful special. Got Big Mama acting strange.
Who were they to command such respect? They
must be people to be feared.

"Pearleane" (that was my grandmother's real
name), "I want Miss Linda here to have a friend
and a playmate," Linda's mother squawked out
the car window in her evangelical voice. "And,
since you've got so many grandchildren under-
foot, I thought we could have one of them during
the day to play with Miss Linda and keep her
company. Do you think you can get one of them
for us now?"

Big Mama looked around the yard nervously
and impatiently. She seemed totally rattled. I
think for the first time she was in a heaping pile
of ants, so to speak, trying to step out of it before

the biting started. She looked around and spotted me.

"Ohhhh, my Lord! Save me!" I said. I had been peeking out from behind an old oak tree in the front yard. My cousins and I played hide-and-seek there. We sometimes pretended we were climbing Jacob's ladder and building a tower to heaven. The tree was just that tall.

At first I could barely hear her calling me. "Gal, come here!"

I hid my body behind the tree, trying with all my might to be still.

"Come here, gal. You hear me calling you."

Her weather-beaten hands took hold of my arms, and before I knew it I was standing in front of Miss Linda. I mean right smack in front of her face.

"Here's one of my grandchildren. Take her. But let me send her over after a while. I just need to clean her up a bit first."

"Wait a minute, here!" I said to myself. "I am cleaned up!"

I couldn't make heads or tails of things. And there was Linda, standing in front of me, inspecting me as though I were a side of beef, trying to determine if I was grade A or throwaway. "She looks all right to me, Mama. I want to play with her now."

"I don't want to send her without a bath," Big Mama said. "It won't take long, ma'am. She'll be right over."

Good Lord, what was going wrong with my

grandmother? Had she lost her mind? I'd just had a bath that morning. And I smelled fine.

That's when it all started. I just knew being friends with this girl was going to cost me my soul. I knew it the moment Big Mama started grappling with her words, crumbling right in front of me. I knew for sure that these people were royalty. And Linda was a princess. I knew I had to conduct myself in a manner worthy of being in her presence, the same way Big Mama did. I knew I couldn't get cross with Linda. Or her family. If by chance I did so, I would, without a doubt, die by their hands. Or they'd make Big Mama kill me.

The next thing I knew I was in my red-and-white polka-dot Sunday school dress with my nice polka-dot socks to match and my black patent-leather shoes that my mom had ordered through the Sears catalog.

There was a burning smell coming from the kitchen. The odor was strong, overpowering. Then Big Mama called me to the kitchen. "Sit down over here," she directed. On top of her black-and-white granite stove was something black, fiercely smoking. My heart landed in my lap.

All I could think was, "Run, run for your life!" I heard Big Mama calling me, but it was a chance I had to take. I couldn't go back. I just couldn't.

I could hear her marching through the house trying to find me. "Marion, come on out. It's not going to burn you. I'm going to be real careful, I promise. You must be pretty when you go to play with Miss Linda."

"Pretty," I said, moving my lips silently. Now how do you think that made me feel? So now I discover I'm not even pretty. I crawled deep under Big Mama's bed, where there were stacks of old boxes filled with whatnots.

She heard the boxes sliding around under the bed. "I'm too old for this kind of foolishness," she said. "Them folks waiting for you, so come on and let me straighten your hair."

Suddenly things were quiet. I could hear her storming out of the house through the front door. Minutes later she was back, tapping on the bed-spread, then on the walls, then the floors. I recognized that sound. It was a switch. She'd gone out front and broke a limb from my oak tree. She pushed the switch under the bed, slapping and swatting it about, until she tagged me several times good, driving me from under the bed.

Now please don't think I went without putting up a kickin' fit. But of course she won.

That straightening comb scared me as much as those strange people did. I smelled of grease and smoke. What was happening to my life—my soul? Tears painted my face as I tried to escape the hot iron. Screams of rage bellowed from deep within me.

"No, Big Mama, don't do this to me," I'd cry out. But there was no end in sight. Day after day, I'd dart to the left and then to the right, each time hoping to escape the pain of this indignity. But to no avail. Burns plastered my ears. My scalp was covered with blisters. My forehead was impaired for life. And all for what?

Linda was intriguing to me. Every day she'd ask about this burn and that burn on my skin. But I never replied. She was always fascinated with the ribbon bows I wore in my hair, asking, "How did you get your hair that way?" Again, I was close-mouthed. I never could explain because I didn't know myself.

The moment came when I decided I would touch her hair and inspect it as she so often did mine. Her silky blond hair swayed like the wind, dancing back and forth across her head and shoulders. I was mesmerized by it. It seemed so nice to have hair that would move so gracefully. Almost floating on air. I said to myself, "Ohhh, so maybe that's what my grandmother is trying to do with mine. Make it dance like the wind. But why did it have to hurt to get it that way?" I inspected Linda for burns. I didn't detect anything remotely resembling a burn. I even cupped a handful of her hair, smelling it for that foul grease and smoke. Again there was nothing. I asked her how she got her hair that way. She looked at me with no reply.

The friendship between Linda and me grew. I began to enjoy the times we spent together—learning to ride horses, exploring the woods that surrounded their sixteen-hundred-acre ranch, fishing, bike riding, going into town with her and her mother, watching her dad smoke meat in a smokehouse . . . I even went to vacation Bible school a couple of times with her.

But I was so tired of dressing up. My patent-leather shoes were killing me. So I started taking them off when Linda and I would play in her dollhouse and putting them back on right when it was time to go home. Linda didn't seem to mind. She didn't seem to mind about anything I did. She was just happy to have me there to play with and be a friend. But I knew Big Mama would have had a fit if she knew how relaxed I'd become around Linda.

Summer passed, and Linda and I were still playing together. But something was beginning to happen to my hair. I was losing it. It was all burnt out. Big Mama was still using the sizzling-hot comb on my hair. Then she heard about perms and decided that there would be no more straightening combs. So she took me to a hairdresser who claimed that she knew how to do it. She put lye, full strength, on my head. My hair stiffened, my head was infested with boils and blisters, my hair stuck to my scalp. We had to get scissors to cut it away from my head. It bled for hours. Within three days it all had come out. I couldn't stand to touch my head or have anyone else touch it.

By the time I was twelve, I was wearing wigs. Wig stores were cropping up all over the place, and Big Mama had bought me one. "You need something to cover your bald head. You don't have enough hair to do anything with, so I bought you a wig to wear."

My heart broke. I knew I would never be whole

again. My life had ended. I was forced to put that wig on my head—hot and uncomfortable. What was a twelve-year-old child doing with a wig on her head? What was it all for?

I began to operate as though the wig were my hair. But I was always afraid that I'd play too hard and it would come off. Or some mean-spirited person would snatch it off.

Sitting next to the wig on my dresser was a small container my grandmother had bought for me marked BLACK AND WHITE OINTMENT: BLEACHING CREAM FOR THE SKIN. Putting it on my face had become a nightly ritual, as had the sweating and burning it caused and having to sleep on my back so the grease would stay on my face and not rub off onto the pillows.

So my grandmother was trying to bleach the black away from my skin. What was going on here, I wondered. Did Linda care about my skin? She never tried to rub the blackness from it. Big Mama would say things like, "It's time for you to use it; it's not too strong for your skin." I wondered what she meant about "it's time."

She was always fixing something on me. Patting here and tucking in there. Pulling and wiping. Still making a fuss over those strange people across the way. And there I was, caught in confusion. Was I ever good? Or was I only as good as what I presented myself to be in this friendship with Linda?

Linda and I had always attended public schools. "Separate but equal." Suddenly I was assigned to her school. But she was no longer there. Her parents took her out and placed her in Sillman's, a private school in a nearby town. She said I was her best friend forever. And I said she was mine. Why couldn't we go to the same school?

Each summer Linda and I continued to play together. We became such friends that her parents began to allow her to break bread at my house the way I did at hers. We never stopped being friends until she wanted to date my brother and my brother wanted to date her, and our friendship, as we knew it, ceased. I'll remember Linda always. I believe she didn't care about the color of my skin as much as Big Mama forced me to care about it.

And now I must live with the struggle of loving myself for who I am, without all the fixing and patting and tucking; without the wiping and the pulling; without the bleaching, without all the hair. I brave the world with my short knots of hair between the scars that are permanent fixtures on my scalp.

Years passed and finally I saw Linda again. Just for a few fleeting moments, we stood side by side in a polling place, waiting to cast our votes. Still blond-haired, blue-eyed Linda. She moved closer to me and whispered in my ear. "Marion," she said, "our doll house is still there. Your name is up there too."

Then she pulled away without saying another word. Tears drenched my soul as I stood there, my heart racing wildly, uncontrollably. My hands jammed against my breasts; it was all I could do to keep from bursting. But I could say nothing. The curtain on the voting booth swung open and I stepped inside. I could feel her watching my every step. Once I was inside the booth, I broke down and wept. Attempts at composing myself were futile. Somehow I managed to cast my vote. I pulled the lever and the curtain swung open. I stepped out and looked for her, but she was gone.

Lost in silence are the hot summer months. Sometimes I feel the strong urge to stop in and say hello. I wonder if she is thinking of me too. I have a feeling she is.

Not a day goes by without me wondering if Linda had an inkling of what I went through to present myself to her. Was she as confused as I was? I believe so. She was caught in something that neither of us had any control over. On some hot summer days I hear her voice. I see her face staring back at mine.

Now I sleep with my comfort quilt pulled tightly over my head. I feel Linda's heart tugging, trying to loosen the quilt's hold on me. Scared of what she will see, what she will know, I need to let her in my comfort quilt because it wasn't she who did this to me.

Linda was my very first playmate. My very first friend. I will never forget my blond-haired, blue-eyed friend. Linda. I long for her still.

J. K. Dennis

———❧———

Born in Milledgeville, Georgia, J. K. Dennis has lived in many places and still travels a lot, "trying to see how other folks live." Currently he is living in Carbondale, Illinois.

In this story from his childhood, J.K. explores the tensions between girls and boys, blacks and whites, in the elementary school he attended. In the surprise ending, we see how one feisty little girl named Margaret Ray was able to change him and his school forever.

SILVER STARS

We all noticed just how different Margaret Ray was when she refused to be punished by Miss Weatherhead. Miss Weatherhead was our teacher. She was a tall white woman with big feet and a big gray hairdo that she lost pencils in all the time. She wore sandals and a pair of black cat-eyed glasses on the edge of her pointed nose. The glasses were attached to a thin gold chain around her neck. Miss Weatherhead would hit us on our hands with a ruler for "misconducting ourselves," as she would call it. She hit so hard that it made the skin inside our hands turn blood red. But Margaret Ray would not let Miss Weatherhead hit her with that wooden ruler for anything in the world.

"Hold out your hand, Margaret Ray Johnson. You have been here at Groover Elementary long enough to know my policy on misconduct."

"No! You ain't gone hit me with that stick."

"Remember, little girls should be seen and not heard," said Miss Weatherhead.

"I'm a woman!" hollered Margaret Ray.

22

This is when Nasty Boy looked at me and I looked at L. Bugg. We knew it was a good thing Margaret Ray was out of our group before she caused any more trouble for us. It would have been different if she hadn't discovered our secret hiding place, which was under Nasty Boy's house in the south end of town. His house stood almost three feet from the ground on stacked concrete blocks. We were having a meeting to see who would collect the money for the ice cream cones that we would buy over at Marvie's. We picked L. Bugg because he was the only one during math hour who could count by threes without pausing to use all of his fingers and other people's fingers who sat close to his desk. Miss Weatherhead always put a little silver star in the middle of his forehead when he got A's on his math tests. Since the busing of blacks to the white school, L. Bugg had been the only one of us to ever get one. He walked around school all day looking like a fool with that silver star on his head. When it refused to stick any longer, L. Bugg pasted it to his forehead with glue. He quit when Nasty Boy and I threatened to kick him out of the group. But he made things just as bad when he sided with Margaret Ray. She was smart to find us squatting under the house, and she would not leave us alone until we let her in our group.

"I know who went over and stole all Miss Tillie's apples off her apple tree, and I know how you been making good marks in math hour too."

"We don't want you in our group!" I screamed.

"You shut up, Jerry Roach. I'll tell your momma you pushed me down and messed up my new dress the other day at school."

"He ain't did no such thing to you at school!" yelled Nasty Boy.

"You shut up, Nathan, or I'm gone tell your momma you throwed rocks at me the other day."

"No he didn't," said L. Bugg.

Then Margaret Ray had to start that fake crying business. Nasty Boy's momma rushed down the steps to the backyard. A long switch was in her hand. Within seconds, she squatted under the house and whipped the switch across our backs and shoulders and legs. We flew away like birds that had been shaken out of a tree. We stood on the sidewalk on the other side of the street listening to Nasty Boy scream for his life. And that was all Margaret Ray's fault too.

It was a two-to-zero vote. L. Bugg and me both decided to hold our meeting deep in the woods by the creek that flowed just off the dirt road that led to Mr. Cooper's house. We tried to swim, but the water stopped above our ankles. We sat in the water on our behinds.

"Ooooooh . . . wee! I'm gone tell. Y'all ain't suppose to be out here." Margaret Ray stood by a tree with her hands covering her eyes. We sat still like dark rocks. "I won't tell if you let—"

"No! You a girl. We don't want no girls in it," I said.

"Okay, then I'm telling." She marched away, dodging tree limbs.

L. Bugg whispered, "Roach, you know what happened to Nasty Boy, and we don't get to see him no more except in school."

At first, it was a one-to-one vote. Then I gave in.

"OK." I stood up. Before I could say anything, Margaret Ray sat behind me in her blue dress.

"You not suppose to wear your clothes in the water, stupid!"

"I ain't stupid! I'm a lady. Move out the way, Jerry Roach. Get over, Leonard Bugg. I want to try to dive in. Move!"

"You can't dive in a creek."

"So!" I said.

"So my big toe, Jerry Roach!" She splashed water in my eyes.

"Stop now! That wasn't a dive. I can dive better than anybody. I been swimming longer than you have anyway, now, 'cause girls can't swim."

"Can too! My uncle taught me how to swim in the Pacific Ocean."

"You a storyteller. She telling a story, L. Bugg."

"Ask my Aunt Sara, then." She raised her nose in the air and stuck out her tongue. It just so happened that Margaret Ray came to live with her aunt, Miss Sara, a month before the busing started. Miss Sara lived around the corner from my house. I wanted to go ask her because I knew Margaret Ray was a big storyteller.

"And when I used to live in Louisiana with my

Aunt Cora, I knew a black man who dived into the Gulf of Mexico."

"You for real?" L. Bugg's eyes were big.

"You can't even spell Gulf of Mexico," I told her.

"Yes I can too."

"What it look like, Margaret Ray? Is it big? What color it is?"

"Shut up, L. Bugg. She can't spell it cause Miss Weatherhead told me our kind have a harder time with words than numbers, and I believe that go double for a girl."

"It is real blue and real cold."

"Everybody know that. Now spell it!" I told her.

"Roach, shut up cause you just mad cause you ain't never been nowhere," said L. Bugg.

"So!"

"Ess oh."

"That don't spell Gulf of Mexico," I told her.

"Where else you been?" L. Bugg made me hot in my face.

"I ain't never dived in it, but I saw Lake Michigan when I used to live up there with my uncle and his mean wife."

"She telling a . . ."

"Shut up and let her talk," said L. Bugg.

"No, 'cause she a storyteller, a big old story-teller."

I stood for a second time. Little chill bumps crawled up and down my arms. I kicked water in L. Bugg's face. He tried to rush me from the side. I swung at him but missed. He fought the air. Margaret Ray jumped on my back and strangled my neck. "Jerry Roach, you better leave Leonard Bugg alone!" She choked my neck and bit my ear so hard that I screamed for my momma. We stopped fighting after I faked death. L. Bugg walked Margaret Ray home like she was some kind of queen. I just sat there in the water thinking about the whole thing and how maybe Miss Weatherhead might not have been right after all.

"Hold out your hand, Margaret Ray. I don't want to have to send you to Mr. Abney's office. Little girls of all colors should be seen and not heard. You have been invited to this school to improve yourself. You do want to be one of the little girls who improves herself, don't you, Margaret Ray?"

"I'm a woman, you stupid lady you!"

Since L. Bugg was so good at math and Nasty Boy and I weren't, Miss Weatherhead gave him permission to move from the back of the class to the middle, right behind Margaret Ray with her storytelling self. She could count a little bit for a girl. But none of us except L. Bugg believed her when she said she could count to a hundred before she was four. Knowing he would get attention, L. Bugg raised his hand.

"Yes, Leonard."

"Is there any math homework tonight?"

"No math homework tonight, Leonard. Now hold out your hand, Margaret Ray." Miss Weatherhead's voice bounced off the walls into every-body's ears.

"No! You ain't gone hit me with no stick, white lady."

"Can you say Miss Weatherhead, Margaret Ray?"

"No, 'cause I hate you and I hate this white school and I hate this white part of town too."

Margaret Ray could not even take a joke. Once I played a joke on Nasty Boy by hiding his clothes in the bushes while he practiced diving in the creek. Nasty Boy then tricked me into believing that the earth was going to be invaded by aliens from Mars, and I couldn't sleep that whole night. I asked Miss Weatherhead in class the next day. It was during quiet hour. I raised my hand. Miss Weatherhead was grading papers at her desk. She had her glasses on, and the gold chain dangled at the sides of her face. She had two yellow pencils sticking out of her hair.

"Yes, Jerry."

"Will aliens be coming here from Mars any time soon, Miss Weatherhead?"

Laughs rolled toward me from every direction. I felt small, with Miss Weatherhead's blue eyes staring at me from behind her glasses. There was no sound for a long time. She frowned too. I could feel the bad coming.

"I can't seem to find your spelling homework here anywhere, Jerry. Did you do it?"

L. Bugg turned around to stare at me. Margaret Ray leaned over to see past L. Bugg's head. Nasty

Boy, who had his head tucked in his folded arms, suddenly popped up and made a fist with one of his hands. I wanted to lie. I had to. But I couldn't. I knew the truth. And I knew Miss Weatherhead knew the truth too but was just waiting to see what I would say. It took me a while before I finally told her no. L. Bugg let out a long breath. Margaret Ray whispered to him how she was going to tell my momma. It seemed like I dropped every book I had and woke the dogs.

"Didn't they teach you all anything at that school! My goodness, that just proves what I have always known. You will never receive a silver star for spelling if you all can't even do homework."

The others in the class snickered. Nasty Boy reached over and punched me on my shoulder for asking such a dumb question in the first place. When he told me I was stupid, I put my head on my desk and cried.

His momma allowed him to join us as we walked down the sidewalk from Marvie's with our ice cream cones. The change that was left rattled in L. Bugg's pocket as he attempted to walk in the exact spots Margaret Ray stepped out of. Nasty Boy switched his chocolate for Margaret Ray's vanilla. Then he let her lead the group home. I tried to protest but Nasty Boy and L. Bugg said they needed some time to like me again, especially after that stupid question about aliens and the extra homework assignments the four of us had to do. They let Margaret Ray do anything she wanted. Then Nasty Boy punched me on my shoulder the same way he did when I asked about the aliens.

"Okay, me and L. Bugg forgive you, so I guess I can tell you the secret now. I stuck something in her ice cream. That's why I traded with her. That'll get her out of our group for good."

"What?"

"I put a dead fly in her ice cream." Nasty Boy pulled L. Bugg out of Margaret Ray's tracks.

"You did it yet?"

"Shush." L. Bugg had a big mouth. Margaret Ray twisted herself around toward us. Chocolate ice cream was around the outside of her lips. Nasty Boy and I both laughed like it was the funniest thing we ever saw.

"Nasty Boy, she probably ate it already," I whispered.

Margaret Ray looked at us and laughed as if she knew what we were giggling and holding our stomachs about. We laughed so much we started faking it.

"What's so funny?"

Ice cream ran down L. Bugg's hand and dripped on the sidewalk, creating little white spots. I stepped forward so I could see Margaret Ray's face.

"A fly was in your ice cream, and you done ate it already, and you gone turn into a fly in your sleep, and you gone look just like one of them aliens from Mars."

"And it was one of them big juicy flies too," said Nasty Boy. He licked his cone on the left and the right and circled his tongue all around it. L. Bugg finally laughed.

"It wasn't no fly in my ice cream."

"Mmm hmmm," I moaned.

"Who did it, Leonard Bugg?" She grabbed the neck of his shirt.

"Don't look at me!" said L. Bugg. "I didn't do it."

I thought the earth was shaking. But I was shaking. Margaret Ray freed L. Bugg, and he tried to lick and look innocent at the same time. Nasty Boy's tongue was rotating back and forth on his ice cream cone. Margaret Ray was the only one shaking. She tried to hold back her tears. Her eyes reddened. They filled with water. Then a tear hit her jaw. She dropped what little was left of her ice cream and ran.

"Look at her, everybody," I said. "She is a big old crybaby. Go on back to the Pacific Ocean. Go on back to the Gulf of Mexico. And you can't even spell it. G-U-L-F-O-F-M-E-X-I-C-O." I licked the ice cream that ran down my hand. Nasty Boy dug into his pocket and pulled out a tiny black something. I squinted my eyes to see if it was what I thought it was. It was.

"That's the fly, ain't it? You said you were going to put it in her ice cream. Nasty Boy, you a story-teller, a big old storyteller," said L. Bugg. L. Bugg dropped his ice cream and swung at Nasty Boy but hit me. L. Bugg had one coming from me any-way, so I rushed him. We both fell backward and thumped against the sidewalk. I couldn't hurt

L. Bugg the way I wanted to because Nasty Boy was on top of us. L. Bugg was stuck in the middle, just as he was when he sat in Miss Weatherhead's class.

"All right, Margaret Ray Johnson! I have had about enough of you for one day." Miss Weatherhead raised the ruler above her head and slammed it down on Margaret Ray's desk. The ruler cracked. Margaret Ray rushed Miss Weatherhead from the side.

"Somebody help me! They are attacking me. John . . . Billy . . . somebody go get Mr. Abney! Hurry!"

We sat with our eyes wide and our mouths open. The chain that was attached to Miss Weatherhead's glasses broke. The glasses cracked as they hit the floor. One of the lenses rolled under Mary Harper's desk. Her pink hands covered both her eyes. Margaret Ray swung and swatted at Miss Weatherhead's face. Miss Weatherhead tried to control her by holding her shoulders, but Margaret Ray twisted and jerked her body so much that poor Miss Weatherhead didn't know what to do besides scream that she had always done good for little black children and that it was unfair for us to be attacking her when all she ever wanted to do was improve us.

"I hate you! I hate you! I hate you! You white lady you! I'm a woman! Nobody hit me with a stick! You stupid lady you! I tried to tell you one time, you stupid lady!"

L. Bugg, Nasty Boy, and I were on the playground about a month later drawing sticks to see who would be responsible for collecting the money to pay for hot fudge sundaes at Marvie's. I looked over at Margaret Ray, who was sitting at the top of the slide. She wouldn't move. Her arms were folded, while the other special children ran wild below her under strict supervision. Then I wondered if she was learning how to spell any big words. Miss Weatherhead retired, and Mrs. Franklin, our new black teacher, told me I was born to spell words. I had made all A's on the spelling test she gave. And, unlike L. Bugg, I wore the silver star that Mrs. Franklin put in the middle of my forehead everywhere I went. I didn't care what anybody said. I wasn't stupid. I was proud of myself.

Toni Pierce Webb

———◆———

Written as a letter to her white great-great-grand-father, "Warmin' da Feet o' da Massa" is part of *Hand-Me-Down Stories*, an unpublished collection that documents seven generations of Toni Pierce Webb's family. The questions she poses in this letter to Massa John are not just personal, she says, but are intended to address the immorality of slavery in general. "If the brutal honesty of the letter is disturbing, it is only because the consequences of slavery are disturbing!"

The mother of four children and the grandmother of five, Toni lives with her husband and two sons in Columbus, Georgia, where she works as a media specialist and librarian. She has had stories for children and stories for adults published, and is currently working on a collection of writings about women entitled *Flashin' and Other Significant Changes*.

WARMIN' DA FEET O' DA MASSA

Any home I've had
Any city I've lived in
Any day of my life

Dear Great-Great-Grandpa Massa John,

Let me begin this letter by telling you that if we, by chance, had ever met, I would not have known what to call you, an affectionate name or Massa John or just plain Massa. Not only are you a stranger to me, but the relationship we share is bizarre. What other American ethnic groups have massas for grandfathers? Do Native Americans or Spanish-Americans have massas for grandfathers? How about Japanese or Irish-Americans—was the white man their massa? Who in this country, besides slaves and masters, shared such an inherently ambiguous and conflicting family structure?

My sisters and brothers and I have known of your relationship with our great-great-grandmother for as long as we can remember. You are as much a part of our genealogical and ethnic heritage as any other ancestor, yet for some reason I have never made my peace with you.

In the past I have been, and sometimes still am, slow to claim you as a forefather. I find it impossible to imagine that you ever felt affection or love for my great-great-grandmother, your captive Missy Pierce. I cannot, no matter how hard I try, envision you as a loving father and grandfather.

Tell me, why did you force yourself upon Missy? (Of course, "force" is putting it genteelly. "Rape" would be a more accurate term.) You had a wife. What sociopathic or neurotic need did you seek to fulfill with my African kin? Was it power over a person whom your sick society told you was not as good as you, less than human? Maybe you were frustrated . . . or was it just simple lust for a black woman? Regardless of your motive, rape was unjustifiable.

Were you cruel toward Missy in other ways, or were you considered a "good master"? Hah! Good master! Now that's an oxymoron if ever there was one. Massa John, only a fool would believe that he could be the master of another human's soul.

How many children of yours did Missy bear? I know only of John, your namesake and my great-grandfather, who was born in August of 1858. Amazingly, his name is John Pierce, like yours, but he does not have the honor of being a junior. He is listed in the 1880 census as a mulatto. You would recognize him anywhere. He carried your genes boldly. Your grandson Sidney, who is my grandfather, also bears the trademark blue eyes, fair skin, and straight hair with which your act of rape burdened him. How did you feel about your first-born son? Did you acknowledge him, love him, accept him—or was he just another Georgia "nigra" to you? Were you proud, ashamed, indifferent? I would love to know!

My memories of my grandmother and grandfather are loving and pleasant, but I often wonder what they thought of you and their other grandfathers—slave holders who raped Granny's and Papa's grandmothers, captives. Was love exchanged between the white fathers and mulatto children and grandchildren? What was the grandfather-grandchild relationship like? Were you affectionate with your eleven grandchildren born of John Pierce and Eliza Maunds Pierce? Did you even know their names?

Massa John, what can you tell me of your relationship with your grandson Sidney R. Pierce, my grandfather? Enlighten me. All I know is that on cold Georgia nights, Papa had to sleep at the foot of your bed to keep your feet warm so you could sleep comfortably.

Massa John, who is to pay for your sins and the sins of others like you? Did you ever consider there would be retribution, payback, judgment, consequences? It's been one hundred and thirty-two years since the Emancipation Proclamation was signed, yet deep-rooted racism and discrimination still permeate this country like an incurable disease. Who pays for your sins, Massa John? We do. I'm sure you do, too.

How should I end this letter, Massa John? Shall I say, "With love, your great-great-granddaughter," or would it be more appropriate to close . . .

With grave misgivings,
Toni Pierce Webb

Sarah Bracey White

———◆◉◆———

When Sarah Bracey White was growing up in Sumter, South Carolina, in the 1950s and 1960s, she could not enter the local public library and could not learn to swim in the town's pool. "By law," she says, "I had to drink from colored only water fountains, sit in the balcony of the local movie theater, and purchase my train ticket out of town at a back window of the white ticket agent's office."

In this story about her first major departure from the south, Sarah takes us on a journey to a girls' camp in Vermont where she was to be a cook's helper for the summer.

After she left the south, Sarah says she believed at first that all white people were the enemy. The events that she describes in this story began a process of opening her mind to the possibility that not all white people were alike. "In my middle age," she says, "an interracial affair made me look beneath the color of a man's skin into his heart. His skin color didn't match my own, but the emotions of his heart did. I married him and we live very happily."

Currently a writer and an arts consultant, Sarah lives with her husband in Valhalla, New York.

FREEDOM SUMMER

In May of 1963, days after my graduation from the segregated Negro high school in Sumter, South Carolina, I received a letter from my favorite aunt, who lived up north in Philadelphia. The envelope contained a sheet of blue-lined notebook paper, a train ticket, a twenty-dollar bill, and a shiny brochure.

Dear Sarah,

I got you a summer job! My friend Claudia Lee from around the corner is the cook at a fancy white girls' camp up in Vermont. She says you can be her helper. The job pays $300 plus train fare, room and board. Wish I coulda had a chance like this when I was your age. I had to pick cotton or take care of white folks' babies. I'm sending you a little spending money for the trip here. See you soon.

Love,
Aunt Susie

P.S. This is a real opportunity!

41

I sure didn't feel that cooking for some white girls was an opportunity! Times were changing for Negroes (that's what we called ourselves then). For me, opportunity was joining the Student Nonviolent Coordinating Committee's lunch-counter sit-ins or marching with Dr. Martin Luther King.

I was only seventeen, but I had a heart full of reasons to hate white people and their restrictive laws: I loved to read, but couldn't use the town library; I paid full admission price to the Sumter movie theater, even though my only access was via a side alley that led to seats in the balcony. My mother's death a few months earlier had increased my bitterness. During one of her frequent asthma attacks, I took her to the Negro wing of the local hospital, where she was injected with numerous drugs and admitted—"only for observation," an intern had assured me. "Asthma doesn't kill you." However, the next morning, a white nurse relayed the news that earlier, they had found my mother dead. "How could you have found her dead?" I screamed. "You were supposed to be observing her! Why'd you let her die? You wouldn't have let her die if she'd been white."

The nurse clenched her mouth in a hard line. "That's unfair," she said.

"You're the ones who're unfair!" I said through quivering lips, then turned and ran from the hospital. I remembered a time before when I had railed about the unequal treatment of Negroes.

My mother had slapped me and, while the tears welled up in my eyes, said, "I did that for your own good—to teach you to control your tongue. Talking like that causes trouble with white folks, and I've already had my share of that."

My older sisters had explained what she meant: Our long-absent father had once challenged the fairness of paying colored teachers less than white teachers, and joined the National Association for the Advancement of Colored People to seek equal pay. He was fired from his principal's job and blacklisted from teaching. Our family lost everything, and he started drinking heavily, then drifted away.

I wanted to continue my father's fight, but Mama was dead, and no matter how much I mourned her death, I had to get on with my life and college was my only way out of South Carolina. I reread my aunt's letter and ground my teeth in frustration. I didn't want a job as a cook's helper. I deserved a job befitting a college girl. I had an acceptance letter from Morgan State University in Baltimore, Maryland. However, the letter made no mention of a scholarship, and my National Defense Student Loan would barely cover tuition, room, and board. I decided to accept the camp job. How bad could it be?

As my train headed toward my Philadelphia rendezvous with Mrs. Lee, I leafed through the brochure my aunt had sent. From its glossy pages, Camp Beenadeewin emerged as a mountain sanctuary—a place that would inspire par-

ents to gladly pay the extravagant sum of six
hundred dollars for their daughters to attend
a three-week session "amidst the marvels of
nature." Horseback riding, archery, arts and
crafts, drama, and swimming in the camp's very
own lake. Swimming appealed to me most.
Negroes weren't allowed in Sumter's public pool,
and Mama's stories about the water moccasins
had kept me away from the muddy pond at the
edge of town; so I'd never learned to swim. But I
wanted to learn, and vowed to do so before the
summer was over. A voice in the back of my mind
intruded on my daydream by asking whether
white people in Vermont were different from
those in Sumter. I used an old civics lesson to
quiet the voice: Northerners had been opposed to
slavery.

Aunt Susie was waiting when I stepped off the
train in Philadelphia. "You look more and more
like your mother," she said as she touched my
cheek. "I'm glad I got a chance to see you before
you left for camp."

I leaned into her embrace and inhaled My Sin
perfume. Mama had worn it too. My chest tight-
ened and my eyes burned, but I held back the
tears and kept my resolve to show my aunt that I
was now a grown-up. We made our way from the
noisy platform into the cavernous station, where
scores of travelers—Negro and white—milled
around the ticket counter or sat patiently on
curved-back pine benches.

Aunt Susie waved at a buxom, caramel-colored woman. "That's Mrs. Lee," she said.

When we reached her side, the woman extended a plump hand. "Hello, Sarah. I'm glad you're going with us. I don't often get college girls to work in the kitchen."

Thrilled to be called a college girl, I beamed as I returned her gentle handshake. "I'll do my best."

"That's all I ask," she said. "No more, no less." She smiled warmly and I smiled back. She sounded just like my teachers at school.

One by one, five more Negro girls arrived and were introduced by Mrs. Lee as the rest of the kitchen help. A brown-eyed, sandy-haired boy of about eighteen arrived as our train was announced. "My name is Charles," he said, and offered to carry one of my suitcases.

When we reached our track, I kissed Aunt Susie and boarded the train. From a window seat, I waved to her. She blew me a kiss and mouthed the words, "God be with you." It seemed like God had abandoned me. I was filled with a mixture of conflicting emotions. The train whistle blew and we pulled away. I busied myself by arranging my suitcases. I couldn't look back. If I did, I knew I'd cry.

"White River Junction, next stop, White River Junction," the conductor announced, swaying from side to side as he navigated the aisle.

"That's our stop," Mrs. Lee said.

I was the last to step from the train onto the wooden platform, which stood like an unfinished bridge in a cool, green clearing. Mrs. Lee and the others had already started down the steep staircase at the end. Birdcalls drifted from the forest that loomed over the one-room station house a few yards away. A hand-lettered sign on its padlocked door read WHITE RIVER JUNCTION STATION HOUSE. Compared to this place, Sumter was a bustling metropolis. The train snorted and pulled away just as a white man beckoned us toward his wood-paneled station wagon.

"Hello, Mr. Henry, how are you?" Mrs. Lee said to the gangly old man who got out and reached for her suitcases.

"Fine, thank you," he replied, while deftly loading the suitcases onto the wagon's overhead rack. "Throw the big stuff up here," he said gruffly, "and I'll tie it down."

The nine of us squeezed inside the station wagon and embarked on the last leg of our journey. Sumter County had few hills and I was unprepared for the gargantuan mountains covered with thick, green forests. Several of the girls dozed, but I stayed alert, feasting on my new environment. I was enthralled by picture-book farmhouses nestled in deep valleys, clouds that looked like smoke rings around distant mountain tops, cows posed on sloping pastures, where rounded boulders sprouted like oversized watermelons. Vermont really was different!

Suddenly, Mr. Henry's voice startled me. "Look to your right and you'll see Camp Beenadeewin." Carved into the valley below, among the trees surrounding a looking-glass lake, was a series of clearings dotted with wooden cabins. Soon we turned onto a road bordered by stately evergreens, then onto one that skirted a lake. My heart leaped at the sight of that shimmering blue water: It was the place where I'd finally learn to swim.

The sun had just dipped to the horizon and filled the sky with a rosy glow when Mr. Henry stopped the car near a wooden building that resembled a grange hall. "Well, folks," he said, "this is it, Camp Beenadeewin—your home away from home for the next seven weeks."

A silver-haired man and a plump, blond woman hurried toward us and embraced Mrs. Lee. After speaking softly to her for a few moments, the woman turned to us. "Welcome to Camp Beenadeewin. I am Mrs. Victoria Winston and this is Mr. Clay Winston. We have owned Camp Beenadeewin for more than thirty years. I'm sure you'll grow to love it as much as Mr. Winston and I do. We are happy you've come to help us care for our lovely campers and counselors. Mrs. Lee has quite a culinary reputation with our girls. I'm sure all of you will help her maintain it."

She then took her husband's arm, and they strolled off.

"Is anybody besides me hungry?" asked Mrs. Lee.

We all raised our hands, as if we were still in school.

"Good," Mrs. Lee said. "While you get settled, I'll whip up something to eat. How's bacon, scrambled eggs, and pancakes with good old Vermont maple syrup?"

We sent up a chorus of yeses.

"Barbara," Mrs. Lee said to one of the girls in our group, "you've been here before—show everybody where things are. Then bring them over to the kitchen."

At the supply house, Mr. Henry issued each of us a set of sheets and two scratchy blankets. Barbara then led the girls to a two-room cabin with three cots in one room and a pair of bunk beds in the other. Chinks in the split-pine wall-boards allowed the setting sun's rays to filter through and settle in ominous shadows across the room. I had a sinking feeling. Everything seemed old and shabby. I wondered if the white girls' cabins were any better than ours. "Where's the bathroom?" I asked.

Barbara walked to a screened window and pointed to a wooden outhouse a short distance away from our cabin. It looked just like the one in my grandmother's backyard. "They don't have indoor plumbing here?" I asked incredulously. Barbara shook her head and pointed to a roofless wooden enclosure. "That's where we shower."

After finishing my first meal and returning to the cabin, I made my bed and climbed into it fully clothed. I pulled both blankets around me, but they weren't enough to warm the chill that invaded my bones. I lay there shivering, knowing that I had made a mistake. I cried quietly, hoping none of the other girls could hear me. I wished I were still home and wondered how I would survive for seven whole weeks.

Mrs. Lee said her homemade cookies were a big favorite with the campers, so before the girls arrived, we had to make enough to last through both sessions of camp. Day after day, we chopped, measured, and mixed ingredients, then rolled, cut, dropped, and baked cookies. The air was filled with the aroma of oatmeal-raisin, sugar, cinnamon, and molasses crisp cookies. Mrs. Lee was a patient but demanding boss, and Charles and I labored under her demands. She had designated Charles as her *chef's assistant*, but he and I worked side by side, learning our way around the big old kitchen, where bowls were the size of drums and the gleaming stainless-steel mixer stood as tall as I did. Each night, I fell into an exhausted, dreamless sleep.

On our fifth day, the white campers began to arrive. Car doors slammed repeatedly, giggles and screams of joyful reunion echoed all around. Charles and I were peeling potatoes and onions for dinner, but I frequently went to the dining-hall door and peered out at the happy chaos. Chauffeurs in dark suits and visored caps unloaded suitcases from the trunks of big black limousines with license plates from places like Pennsylvania, New York, Connecticut, and Massachusetts.

Some campers were accompanied by young, well-dressed mothers who looked like they had never lifted anything heavier than a cup of tea. My mother had wanted a life like I imagined they lived—a pampered life as the wife of a successful man. She thought she'd found such a life with my father. It probably would have been, too, if he hadn't run afoul of the white establishment.

"These girls actually seem happy to be coming to a place like this," I said to Charles. "I can't imagine anybody paying six hundred dollars to spend three weeks in a raggedy place like this."

Charles chuckled. "All year long, these girls live in mansions—with maids and butlers. They think this place is exciting. Gives them a chance to be on their own and *commune with nature*, like the brochure says." He guffawed. I laughed too, as I recalled my last trip to the outhouse, where I found a raccoon curled up on the floor.

"I hate it here," I said, sobering up. "Mrs. Lee says we can't go in the lake, or ride the horses or anything. It's as bad as being in South Carolina. I thought it was different up north."

Charles dumped a ten-pound bag of onions into one tub of the big steel sink and turned on the cold water. "It is. You don't have to worry about having your head bashed in for looking a white person in the eye. And you get paid for your labor."

I grunted, picked up an onion, and began to peel off its thin brown layers, grateful that I could cry without anyone asking why. Maybe we were getting paid, but it sure wasn't any better than life in South Carolina.

Camp shifted into full swing and our days were

filled with preparing, serving, and cleaning up after meals. Before coming to Beenadeewin, I had never done domestic work, so I found it strange to serve these young white girls. Mrs. Lee said I was to address each camper and counselor, whatever her age, as Miss. I said the word only when she was within hearing. None of the campers called me anything except "girl," and they said that only when they wanted more of something: "*Girl*, you! Bring me some more milk." "*Girl*, bring me some more butter." "Some more gravy, *girl*." God, how I hated that tone.

When I asked Mrs. Lee why we couldn't ride the horses or swim in the lake, she had smiled sadly and said, "We're the help, and up here, the help doesn't mingle with the campers." Up north, it seemed segregation was a matter of class as well as skin color.

Even though it wasn't my job to serve the tables, I helped out wherever I was needed. At first, some campers stared curiously (didn't their rich parents tell them it was impolite to stare?); others pointed and whispered; a few treated me as if I were their personal servant. Occasionally, one muttered "thank you" when I proffered fresh water, napkins, or refilled dishes.

Always, I felt them examining me, as if I were a strange laboratory animal. Couldn't they see that I was just like them? I wanted to tell them that in a few months I would be in college studying to become a French translator at the United Nations. I wanted to show them the medal I won for writing the best news story in any high school paper (Negro or white) in the whole state of South Carolina. I wanted to tell them that I had been elected to the National Honor Society and show them the tiny gold-and-black pin I'd been awarded. Instead, I buttered slices of toast as they dropped off the revolving toaster rack, pressed them into the plate of cinnamon sugar, and pretended it didn't matter what they thought of me.

However, even though I hated the way they studied me, I was shamelessly curious about them. Never before had I been in such close proximity to so many white girls my own age. Day by day, eavesdropping grew easier as they got used to my "brown" presence. No one worries about a pine tree hearing secrets, and I became about as significant as a pine tree. Listening to their conversations, I learned that white skin brought no solace from problems; that money did not prevent sadness and heartache; that white girls were cruel to each other (I had always assumed that whites were only cruel to Negroes); that most white girls want to be blond and would die for the perfect tan. The last discovery gave me a lot to think about. Why, since they didn't even like brownskinned people, would they want to have skin like mine?

Six days a week, I followed the same schedule: up by 5:30 a.m. and straight into the kitchen. After breakfast was served, I had a two-hour break before starting lunch; after lunch, another two-hour break before dinner. We made everything the campers ate, and it was backbreaking work to prepare such large quantities of food, day after day. My only pleasure was eating.

During a lull in breakfast one morning, Mrs. Lee pointed out a corner table where the counselors ate. Most of them seemed to be my age or a little older. "They're all college girls, like you," she said. "Mrs. Winston thinks college girls set a good example for the young campers."

"They're not college girls like me," I answered. "They're white. And I'll bet they're making more money than I am, for a lot less work."

Mrs. Lee shrugged. "That's how life is."

I couldn't understand why adults just accepted everything. Just because that's the way it's always been doesn't mean that's the way it has to be. I knew that when I got to be an adult, I would do whatever I could to change things.

Every Sunday, after the kitchen crew served breakfast and lunch, and prepared box suppers for the campers, Mr. Henry took us sightseeing. After a few Sundays of becoming "the sights" for the locals, I grew reluctant to join the tour. But there was nothing else to do, so I'd go, forcing myself to ignore the stares, pretending that I was a tourist on vacation. The only trip I looked forward to was the one to Montpelier, the state capital, where I expected to see others who shared my skin color. When we didn't, I surmised that we were the only Negroes in Vermont. No wonder everyone stared at us.

We took a guided tour through the atrium of

the state capitol building, where I noticed sea-
shells embedded in the marble floor. The guide
said they were prehistoric fossils, left behind
when glaciers carved their way across the land.
I wondered what I could leave behind as proof
that I had been in Vermont, proof for the next
Negroes that someone like them had been here
before.

The guide talked about the spirit of hard work
and self-denial that marked Vermonters, and I
began to understand the austerity at Camp
Beenadeewin. Back home, Negroes strove to gain
the material things that Vermonters could easily
have but shunned. To them, matters of principle
were more important. Matters of principle were
important to me too. I had hated it when clerks at
Belk Stroman Department Store left my mother
unserved while they waited on all the white
folks, even those who arrived after us. I'd hated
standing in the rear of a bus while empty seats
abounded in the front—seats reserved for whites
only. Those things branded me as inferior, though
I knew I wasn't, and I wanted to change them. I
was ashamed that I was in Vermont, instead of at
home, crusading to make southerners change
their ways.

After meals, while the other girls who worked
in the kitchen cleaned up and washed dishes,
Charles and I usually sat at a picnic table and
talked. He'd never been south of Philadelphia,
and I told him about life below the Mason-Dixon

line. He couldn't understand why Negroes stayed in the south, since whites treated them so badly there. I repeated the explanation my mother had offered when I urged her to leave Sumter: "You can love a place and want to stay there, even though it's not perfect."

"That's crazy," Charles said. I smiled, remembering when I had voiced that exact sentiment to my mother.

Mid-July, four weeks after our arrival at Camp Beenadeewin, the first set of campers left and I was free until the second set arrived two days later. I had declined to join the Sunday tour and was alone in the cabin. The afternoon air was hot and still. Sweat beaded up all over me and I was miserably uncomfortable. I decided to go for a walk near the lake, even though I'd been warned that it was off-limits to kitchen help.

The well-worn path to the lake took me through a stand of pine trees, where brown needles cushioned the cool pathway. I considered staying there in the shade, but the persistent gnats and summer flies made me press on. When the path neared the lake, it widened and descended a sharp bank. I stopped, overpowered by the lake's beauty and size. I shaded my eyes against the afternoon sun. The lake extended as far as I could see. Tall trees cloaked in feathery foliage protectively surrounded it. To my right, several rowboats were tied to a wooden dock. To my left, the pathway disappeared into the lake. I swatted a mosquito on my arm and scratched at the resulting sting. It was minor, compared to the deep sting that tortured my heart. I wanted to cry.

What gave these white people the right to keep me from going into this lake? They didn't make it. God did. And He made it for everybody. Surely there was room for me to enjoy its coolness. I removed my sandals, then walked down the bank. At the water's edge, I stopped. What if someone saw me? The thought of getting caught chilled my bravery. I looked around, but saw no one.

Still, I was afraid. My heart beat faster and I could almost hear Mama's voice. "Sarah, don't make trouble. Put on your shoes and go back to that cabin right now!" I ignored the voice and waded in. The sun was hot against my top half while my feet and legs were icy cold. It was a tantalizing feeling. I squished the mud on the bottom between my toes and a cloud swirled around my feet.

I listened for sounds, but all I heard were chickadees chirping and squirrels rustling through the trees. I lifted my skirt and waded farther out. The water was now midway to my thighs. I shivered with delight, tucked my skirt in my waistband, and bent to splash water on my mosquito-bitten forearm. Suddenly, I was angry. Angry at all the campers, at all the white people in Vermont. Angry at their selfishness, at the unfairness of life, which showed me its bounty but denied me access. Angry at myself for my helplessness and fear.

I began to cry and strike at the water with my

palms. I wanted to punish these people. But how? Then it came to me. Since they thought I was going to contaminate their beautiful lake, I would. Slowly and deliberately, I waded back to the water's edge, lowered my cotton panties, squatted down and peed. I watched my urine flow into the lake and felt a sense of satisfaction. I had made my own mark on that vast, beautiful place.

After a while, I collected my sandals and headed back to my cabin. As I approached the stand of pine trees, a young woman with a long blond ponytail stepped out from behind a tree and blocked my path. "Why did you do that?" she asked.

I stared into her big blue eyes and defiantly answered, "Because I wanted to." I tried to pass her, to reach the safety of the cabin, but she thrust out a freckled arm and stopped me. "Let me pass," I said.

"If I tell Mrs. Winston, you'll be in big trouble," she answered.

"You can tell whoever you want. I don't care," I said. But I did care. My heart was doing flip-flops and my blood was pounding in my ears. What would Mrs. Lee say? And Aunt Susie? I had let them down. Would I be sent home in disgrace? Would I lose all the money I had endured such hardship to earn? A sense of doom settled around my heart.

"If you don't care, why do you look so scared?" the girl asked.

I thought I saw amusement in her eyes. That made me so angry it overpowered my fear. "You startled me," I said, mustering the calmest voice I could. "I didn't think anyone was around."

"There's always somebody around this place when you do something you're not supposed to do," she said.

Suddenly, this mocking girl embodied all the white people who stood between me and what I wanted to do. I shouted at her, "What gives anybody the right to say I'm not supposed to come down to this lake? Or swim in it?"

She laughed. "What you were doing wasn't swimming."

I folded my arms and raised my chin. I wouldn't let her see my fear. "Are you going to let me pass or what?"

"Don't you want to know if I'm going to report you?"

"I don't care what you do," I answered haughtily, though I couldn't banish the tremble I felt in my voice.

"That's not true. You wouldn't be working here if you didn't need the money. If I tell Mrs. Winston, you'll be in big trouble."

"So are you gonna tell her?"

Suddenly, the girl collapsed into giggles. "Everybody pees in the lake. They just don't make a pilgrimage to do it."

I didn't laugh with her. Maybe she thought this was a joke, but I didn't.

"I've seen you in the dining hall," she said,

regaining her composure, "watching us. You're always so serious. Don't worry, I won't tell. It'll be our little secret."

"Don't expect me to thank you," I answered, ungraciously.

"Why are you so angry? I'm trying to be nice to you."

"Why am I angry?" I repeated, surprised by the indignation in my voice. "Wouldn't you be angry if they brought you here and kept you penned up like an animal? Everything at this camp is off-limits to me, except the kitchen!"

The girl stared at me, but said nothing. She looked appropriately dismayed. That pleased me and diluted my anger. "I'm not as angry as I should be," I said. "If I were, I would have burned this whole place down, instead of peeing in the lake."

"But that would hurt you too," she said.

Her words sounded sincere, but I was suspicious. "Why do you care?"

"Has it ever occurred to you that all white people don't dislike you?"

"No, it hasn't," I said.

"I don't dislike you," she said softly.

Uncomfortable with her words and the emotion in her voice, I wanted to run back to the safety of my cabin. "Does that mean you're going to let me by?" I asked. She stepped aside and gestured for me to pass. I could feel her eyes following me. After a few steps, I turned back and mumbled, "Thank you." I sprinted back to my cabin, flung myself on my cot, and lay there trembling. Mama had always said you couldn't trust white folks. "They'll lie to you with a smile on their lips," she had said. Was she right? Would this white girl betray me?

The next morning while we prepared breakfast, I told Charles what had happened at the lake.

He guffawed loudly. "I can't imagine prim little you lifting up your dress and peeing in Lake Beenadeewin," he said, then added in a singsong voice, "What would your Mama say to that?"

I narrowed my eyes and stuck my tongue out at him.

"Hey, I like the idea. Sorta like the way dogs mark their territory. Maybe I'll go do it too."

"This isn't funny, Charles. I'm scared she's going to tell somebody and get me in a whole lot of trouble."

He shrugged. "Well, the die's cast—so to speak," he said, grinning. "You'll just have to wait and see what she does."

Later, as I stacked bread on the toaster racks, I looked across the serving counter into the same blue eyes I had seen the previous day. My heart flip-flopped.

"Good morning," she said. "May I have two slices of cinnamon toast?"

I placed the toast on a plate and slid it across to her.

"My name's Sharon," she said. "What's yours?"

"Sarah," I replied, without looking at her.

"Stop looking so scared, Sarah. I told you your secret's safe with me." She flashed me a smile, then returned to the counselors' table.

Was I really safe? Maybe Mama hadn't been right about all white people.

"Sarah, go stir the Maypo before it sticks to the bottom of the pot," Mrs. Lee called to me. "The next round of campers will be coming in soon."

A day later, between lunch and dinner, as I sat at our picnic table waiting for Charles, I heard twigs cracking and looked up to see Sharon approaching. What did she want?

"Sarah," she said, "can I talk to you?"

"About what?" I asked suspiciously.

"Nothing in particular. Just talk."

I shrugged and looked around, hoping Charles would come out and rescue me from this awkward encounter.

"Is it okay if I sit down?" she asked.

I shrugged again. "It's not my picnic table," I said grudgingly, not wanting to encourage her.

Sharon straddled the bench on the other side. "Where are you from?"

"South Carolina."

She laughed. "So that explains your funny accent."

"What funny accent?" I said defensively, wishing Charles would show up.

"You talk different from Mrs. Lee and the other girls in the kitchen."

"They're from Philadelphia."

"The guy too?"

"Charles? Yeah, he's from Philadelphia, too."

"My college roommate is from there. She calls it Philly. You'd like her."

"Is she a Negro?" I asked, implying that that would be the only reason I might like her roommate.

If Sharon got my meaning, she didn't let on. "No, she's not. But you'd like her anyway."

"You don't know what I'd like," I said curtly. "You don't know anything about me."

Sharon gave that amused smile that really irritated me. "I know enough about you to know you'd like her. She's got your spunk. Always in trouble for saying what she thinks. I wish I could be like that."

"Like what?" I asked. "In trouble, or saying what you think?"

"You don't have to take offense at everything I say," Sharon said testily. "It was meant as a compliment."

As I looked at the angry pout her lips formed, I realized that Sharon was treating me like an ordinary human being, the way I wanted white people to treat me, but I was acting like an angry animal.

"I'm sorry," I said. "My mother always told me my mouth would be the death of me. Every year I make a resolution to talk less, but I never keep it more than a few days."

"I don't think you talk much at all—though

sometimes you do say mean things." She flashed a mock stern expression that made furrows between her eyebrows. Then she softened. "My resolution is always to talk more, especially about things that matter. I don't do that either."

"I'm curious about something," I said. "Why didn't you tell anyone what you saw me do at the lake?"

Sharon's face grew serious. "I didn't see anything so very wrong with what you did. If they kept me out of the lake, I'd want to do the same thing. Somebody ought to tell Mrs. Winston that what she's doing is wrong. Things are changing in the world today."

What was this girl saying? Was she planning a protest march up here? I thought wryly. "I don't think this is the time for people to start keeping resolutions," I said. "Not if they want to keep their jobs."

From the corner of my eye, I spotted Charles standing at the edge of the dining hall and waved for him to come over. "Sharon, this is Charles. Charles, this is Sharon. I told you about her."

"What did she tell you about me?" Sharon asked as she extended her hand to Charles.

To my surprise, Charles took her hand in his, bent forward, and brushed her fingertips with his lips. "Just that you walk softly and carry a big stick," he said.

"She's only half right," Sharon said.

"Which half?" he asked.

Sharon grinned. "You'll have to find out for yourself."

Uncomfortable with their banter, I interrupted. "Isn't it time for us to get back to work, Charles?"

He nodded. "That's why I came to get you, but I was distracted."

Sharon giggled. "I've got to get back to work too. Maybe we can do this again." I hope not, I said to myself. "What was that all about, Charles?" I asked as soon as we reached the kitchen.

"Drama."

"Drama?"

"Yeah, drama. She's the drama teacher."

"How do you know?"

"I did a little snooping after you told me she saw you at the lake."

"And what's hand kissing got to do with drama?"

"Why, Sarah, do I detect jealousy in your voice?"

"I'm not jealous!"

"You don't need to be. You're my friend and I wanted to help you. I figured if I could get on her good side, maybe I could keep her from telling anybody. Since she teaches drama, she must like acting. I saw Cary Grant do that hand-kissing bit in a movie."

"I don't think I have to worry about her telling anybody," I said. "But you'd better worry about kissing white girls' hands. Where I come from,

Negro boys don't do that. Not if they want to grow up to be men."

"We're not down south, Sarah."

"Doesn't matter. Things are the same all over."

"No, they're not, " he said. "That's why the Freedom Riders are going south."

"What do you mean you never talked to a white person before me?" Sharon asked, her voice heavy with disbelief.

"I've talked to them," I answered, "but only when I was buying something in a store. Never like this, except once."

"What did you talk about then?"

"Rip."

"Who's Rip?" she asked.

I hesitated. I hadn't even told Charles about Rip. "Rip was my dog," I finally said. "I named him after Rip van Winkle because he slept a lot when I first got him. One day when I came home from school, I couldn't find him. I cried and cried. About a month later, I saw him in a lady's yard, not far from our house. When I told her he was my dog, she said if I wanted him back, I had to pay for his vet's bill and the food she'd fed him.

"My mother said she didn't have money for that, so I told her to get the sheriff to make the lady give him back. She told me that the sheriff was white, just like the lady, and since it was only our word against hers that Rip was my dog, the sheriff would side with the white lady."

Sharon stared solemnly at me, tears shining in her eyes. "Did you get him back?"

"No."

"Is that why you hate white people?"

"I don't hate white people," I said, then added, "At least, not all of them."

"That was a rotten thing for that woman to do," Sharon said. "I'd hate her too. What did she look like? I want to picture her while I hate her now."

I tried to remember what the woman looked like. All I could recall was that she was white. "I can't remember," I admitted.

"I'd never forget the face of the person who stole my dog," she said. "Not ever."

Sharon was right. As much as I hated that woman, I shouldn't have forgotten what she looked like. She was a cruel person, but only one person, not a whole race of people. I had been wrong to substitute her skin color for her crime.

"Tomorrow the campers leave," Sharon said, as we sat at the picnic table our last afternoon together.

"And we're leaving the day after that," I said. "I can hardly wait."

"Haven't you gotten to like Camp Beena-deewin, even a teeny little bit?" she asked.

I looked up at the trees that towered around the compound. Thanks to Sharon, I could identify them as sugar maples, white birch, eastern hemlock, and chestnut. Still, I longed for oak, pecan, and chinaberry trees . . . even the mulberry tree, which each summer litters the ground beneath its fuzzy green leaves with fat, purple berries that stain everything they touch. Trees that held memories for me. Trees that I would always recognize, whatever the season. "It's been an experience," I said finally. "I learned a lot, and I met you."

"Will you tell your friends about me?" she asked.

"I don't know," I said. "Will you tell your friends about me?"

"I've already written my roommate about you. She wrote back that she's thinking about becoming a Freedom Rider."

A white girl risking her life to get equal rights for Negroes? Would wonders never cease? It had taken a trip to Vermont for me to discover what white people *could* be like. I looked closely at Sharon, trying to memorize her face. I wanted to remember it, so that she would not blend into the faceless mass of white people who inhabited my past. Mostly, I would remember her blue eyes and the way they changed color when she was sad or angry, and her eyelashes—so pale they were almost silver. But I also would remember the way she pressed her lips tightly together when she was tense or amused and trying not to laugh, and the way her cheeks reddened when she blushed. And I would remember that, like me, she bit her nails, which we both resolved to stop.

Mrs. Winston waved as Mr. Henry started the engine. "Good-bye, girls. Thank you for all your hard work. I hope you'll come back next summer."

Not if I can help it, I said to myself. When we reached the road that circled the lake, I spotted Sharon walking alone. When we passed her, she turned toward the car, our eyes met, and she waved. I waved back.

"You know that girl?" Mrs. Lee asked.

"A little," I answered, "just a little." But not nearly enough, I thought. Sharon had made me reconsider a lot of things my mother had taught me—things Mama had thought necessary for my survival. But so much was changing in my world. Since I wanted to change the way white people thought about me, maybe I needed to change the way I thought about them. As the station wagon pulled on to the evergreen-lined road out of camp, I looked back with mixed feelings. I would never *love* Camp Beenadeewin the way Sharon did, but I had learned a lot of things during my stay there. Things that would affect my life forever.

Dianne E. Dixon

A civil rights attorney, Dianne Dixon lives in a brownstone in Bedford-Stuyvesant, the area of Brooklyn, New York, where she was born in the late 1950s.

"My writing informs who I am as much as my gender, my race, and my profession," she says. "My experiences during sixteen years as a black female civil rights attorney permeate my writing, and my work tends to spotlight themes of social justice and personal responsibility."

Dianne says that her experiences with race relations have been "overwhelmingly negative. I developed a deep distrust of white people from being mistreated by my teachers and fellow classmates when I attended a predominantly white school for the first time." Perhaps partially as a consequence of the discrimination that Dianne recounts in her story, she is a strong advocate of affirmative action. But she is careful to define it accurately. "Too many people are of the belief that affirmative action means that those less qualified will be given jobs, promoted, or admitted into schools based solely on their race or gender, giving rise to the concept of 'reverse discrimination.' But, this is not what affirmative action is about. Rather, affirmative action simply authorizes an employer or educator to consider race as one factor in making decisions on hiring or admissions."

An accomplished attorney and writer, Dianne is also a writing teacher and the assistant director of the John Oliver Killens Writers' Workshop. She currently teaches legal writing at New York University and is working on her first novel, *How Sweet the Sound*.

THE LESSON

Often when I sit down to write, I am transported momentarily back to the sixth grade. It was 1969. One year earlier, Dr. Martin Luther King Jr., had been murdered, and fifteen years before that, the United States Supreme Court had delivered the landmark *Brown v. Board of Education of Topeka* decision. Throughout the country, people were protesting against racism while black children were being attacked on school buses for having the audacity to attend white schools.

In Bedford-Stuyvesant, Brooklyn, where I lived, racism was something that I had only seen on TV or heard about in my parents' stories of growing up in the south. I had graduated from an all-black elementary school two blocks from my home, where the majority of my teachers were black and their expectations that I and my classmates would succeed had been both obvious and uplifting. In the school where I attended sixth grade, every-thing changed.

It seemed like my mother had called every school official in the city to make sure I got into that school. I overheard her explain to my aunt, "Dianne is a bright girl. That school is the nearest one to us with a program for gifted kids. I know it's a long ride on the bus, and I know she will have to get up real early to get there on time. But they have smaller classes and newer equipment—and why shouldn't our kids get the best that's out there?" So, with little fanfare, I boarded the city bus alone every day and rode for fifty minutes to a predominantly white school, in an all white neighborhood, with all-white teachers. Mr. Perlman was one of those teachers, and I still remember the lessons he taught me.

"Well, Miss Dixon, I had hoped that you would do better than this," Mr. Perlman sneered as he handed me back my writing assignment. The bright red F on the first page of my paper was so large that I was sure everyone in the class had seen it. An F. An F! I had never gotten an F before. I shoved my paper inside my notebook and tried not to look around to see who was watching me. I knew, of course, that Nancy Cicero had seen the F. How could she miss it? She was sitting right next to me.

"Good job, Nancy!" Mr. Perlman made a point of saying as he handed Nancy back her paper with a normal-sized B+ on it.

"Thank you, Mr. Perlman," she said. And then, turning to me, she said, "I didn't think I was going to do well on this paper at all. I didn't write it until the night before we had to hand it in. What did you get, Dianne?"

"A headache," I answered, turning my head to look out the window.

"Those of you who received a D or lower, please see me after the bell rings," Mr. Perlman announced, looking directly at me.

"Well, I guess you'll have to stick around, won't you, Dianne?" Nancy laughed.

"Drop dead, Nancy," I shot back.

I waited to see who the other kids with bad grades would be, gathering around Mr. Perlman's desk. But only one kid remained with me. It was Nat, the only other black kid in my class. I didn't know what I would have done had I not had him to talk to. The kids in the other classes—even the few black ones—hated us for being in the gifted program. And the kids in our gifted class acted like we didn't exist. It was because of Nat that I tried to ignore my Sunday night headaches and the nosebleeds that I so often got on Monday mornings. And it was because of him that I tried never to be absent from school. I couldn't do that to Nat, and I knew he wouldn't do it to me. We both had perfect attendance records.

After class I asked Mr. Perlman what I had done wrong on the assignment.

"Well, for one thing, you didn't write on the topic I assigned the class. Do you remember what it was supposed to be?"

"Yeah, I remember," I said. "You told us to write an essay about an event in our lives that changed the way others viewed us."

"And what did you write about?"

I told him what he already knew, that I had written about the double-Dutch contest between me and my friend Charlene the preceding summer.

He became agitated. "You see? You see what I mean? Now what has *that* got to do with the assignment I gave? You write about a rope jumping contest which, I might add, you didn't even win."

"No, I didn't win it," I agreed, "but I was new on the block and when I stood up to Charlene's rope-jumping challenge everybody stopped thinking of me as an outsider."

My explanation had not moved Mr. Perlman. He just sucked his teeth and rolled his tiny blue eyes at me. "Listen, Dianne, if you intend to pass this class, you are going to have to do the assignments properly. And that goes for you, too, Nathaniel. Your grammar is pathetic, surpassed only by your atrocious spelling."

Nat said nothing. He just stared at Mr. Perlman, but I could see he was mad.

"I want the two of you to read chapters seven through nine in your writing textbooks and answer the questions at the end of each chapter. Maybe by reading some information on essay writing, you'll get it. Now, tomorrow I'm going to ask a few of the students to read their essays to the class to illustrate the proper way the assignment should have been done. Be sure to listen carefully. In fact, I'll be doing this for the rest of the school year, so you'll get to hear lots of good writing."

Nat and I tried to ignore the fact that Mr.

Perlman was really telling us that he thought we could never write anything good enough to read to the class, and that all we could ever hope to do well was listen. In the hall, as we walked to our lockers, Nat exploded. He hated Mr. Perlman for always picking on us. He seemed to enjoy telling people on the sly how Nat and I didn't belong in the gifted program. The fact that both of us had been in gifted classes our entire school lives and that we performed well above average on every test put in front of us seemed to escape him.

The next day, instead of waiting until the end of class, Mr. Perlman asked for the homework assignment he had given Nat and me as soon as everybody had taken their seats. With everyone watching, we had to walk up to Mr. Perlman's desk and hand in our work. We both knew that Mr. Perlman wanted to embarrass us, but I refused to give him the satisfaction. I held my head up high, put a smile on my face, and handed him the homework, saying, "Here, Mr. Perlman. It really helped. Thanks." Watching his face turn red made my smile genuine.

Before Nat and I could return to our seats, Mr. Perlman told the class that he was giving another writing assignment. "I want to see those creative juices flowing," he said. "There is no particular topic on which you must write, which should make the assignment easier for some of you," he said, looking directly at me. "All papers are due on Monday, so you have the entire weekend to create your masterpiece. Are there any questions?"

When no hands went up, Mr. Perlman began the day's exercise. But I didn't listen to anything he was saying. I was excited about the opportunity to show Mr. Perlman how I could write. Since no specific topic was required, nothing I wrote could be wrong. Here was my chance, and Nat's too, to prove to Mr. Perlman and the class that we belonged there. Maybe then Mr. Perlman would treat us like the other kids.

After school I asked Nat what he was going to write about. He wrinkled his face and shrugged his shoulders like he was trying really hard to come up with an answer. Then he smiled. "I don't know, Dianne, but maybe I'll write a murder mystery with Mr. Perlman as the corpse."

I shook my head. I really wanted to come up with a good topic. Nat was somewhat less enthusiastic. "You know, whatever we do, Mr. Perlman is going to hate it."

But I insisted that this time had to be different. "This time we can write anything. If we just double-check our grammar and spelling—"

"—Why do we have to dot every *i* and cross every *t*?" Nat interrupted me.

He had a point, but I was certain that if we did a good job on the paper Mr. Perlman would not have any excuse to treat us differently from the rest of the class.

Nat just looked at me and said nothing.

By the time I reached home I had my topic. I had seen twin girls on the bus. They made me wonder what it would be like to have a twin, and so I decided to write about twin sisters. I shouted a hello to my mother and ran to my room to change my clothes and begin writing. At first, all I could do was stare at the paper and chew my pencil eraser. I knew I wanted to write something about twin sisters, but what exactly? At dinner that night I stared at my plate, mad at myself for not having come up with an adventure for my twins.

I barely heard my father speaking to me. "Dianne, that food on your plate did not do a thing to you, so why are you giving it such a dirty look?"

"I'm not that hungry, Dad."

He looked at my mother for explanation, but she offered none. "Are you feeling okay, Dianne?"

"Yeah, I'm okay. I'm just thinking about something," I said.

"Uh-huh. Well, try eating some of those black-eyed peas on your plate. Don't you know that black-eyed peas are good for thinking?" He teased me further. "Yeah, black-eyed peas—not fish—is the real brain food."

"Black-eyed peas, huh, Daddy?"

"That's right. I heard tell that George Washington Carver himself used to eat a bowl of black-eyed peas every day. That's how come he was able to make his discoveries about the peanut and the sweet potato. A lot of people don't know that."

"I bet they don't," I said, laughing and scooping up a forkful of the new brain food. Then it hit me. Why not make my twins geniuses like George Washington Carver? Why not have them discover something, as he did? I quickly finished my dinner, making sure to eat my black-eyed peas, and rushed back to my room. This time, when I sat down to write, the words began to flow. I wrote for hours, until I was so sleepy I had to go to bed.

I spent Sunday, after church, cleaning up my grammar and spelling. I wasn't going to let Mr. Perlman use that excuse to keep from giving me an A.

Monday morning, Nat was waiting for me in front of the school building when I got off the bus. We exchanged stories, sitting on the steps. His story was good, and what impressed me even more was that Nat said it was true. He had written about his grandparents, who were threatened by the Ku Klux Klan after refusing to sell their land in South Carolina to a white farmer who wanted it, but they were able to defend themselves and keep their land.

I asked Nat what he thought of my story. When he told me that he really liked it, I thought we both had Mr. Perlman this time.

We hurried into the building to beat the late bell. That was probably the first time that I had actually looked forward to Mr. Perlman's class. But by the time the bell rang, I began to have some doubts. I kept thinking of different ways I could have written my story. We barely had a chance to take our seats before Mr. Perlman demanded our assignments. He announced that he would return them that Friday. Great! All I had to do was make it to Friday.

The week just dragged. Nat kept telling me not to worry, that we were sure to do well. But nothing he said could make the sickly feeling in my stomach go away. The more I tried to put the story out of my mind, the more I thought about nothing else. Every day I tried to read the expression on Mr. Perlman's face for some clue about whether he had read and liked my story. Was he smiling at me or was that a sneer? It was hard to tell with his thin lips. Finally, Friday came.

Nat made a point of telling me that we were going to get our papers back that day. I rolled my eyes at him. Like I needed him to remind me about Friday. I asked him what grade he thought we would get on our papers. He frowned for a moment and then laughed. "Knowing Mr. Perlman, I bet he didn't like me putting down the Ku Klux Klan. And in your story the black girls are smart, which he probably didn't like either, so we'll both only get C's. But, hey, a C is better than an F."

I didn't laugh.

When the bell rang, my heart jumped. This was it. I stared at Mr. Perlman's face as I entered the classroom. Was he happy, upset, aggravated, excited? I couldn't tell. I took my seat next to Nancy Cicero and waited for the verdict.

"Settle down, please, everyone. I have your papers to return, and I must say there were some interesting stories from some of you. Of course, others showed no improvement at all."

Was he looking at me when he said that?

He walked around the classroom, handing back the papers and making his usual comments. "Well done, Rebecca. George, watch your spelling. Nice job, Nancy."

Nancy smiled and laid her story on her desk to make sure I saw her B.

Mr. Perlman gave Nat back his story without saying a word. Nat looked at his paper and shrugged. Then he looked at me, holding up the title page to show me the C+ scribbled across the top. We both knew that Nat deserved better. There was not one red mark for grammar or spelling corrections, so why the C+? I shook my head and frowned. Things didn't look good for me, and I began to get angry.

When Mr. Perlman walked to the front of the classroom to announce the names of the students who would read their work to the class, I was surprised. He hadn't given me back my paper yet. I wondered how it could be so bad that he wouldn't even return it, but then I remembered that he had given me back my other assignment with the huge red F on it without blinking an eye. So where was my paper now? When he called out my name, I sat frozen. He had included me with the students who would read their papers to the class.

Nancy Cicero's mouth dropped open. She seemed to be more in shock than I was.

I watched as, one by one, the four other kids whose names had been called before mine read their stories. I watched them, but I couldn't listen to them read. I was too excited.

I was going to read my story to the class! He wanted me to read my story to the class! I was glad that I had put so much work into the writing.

Mr. Perlman stood, holding out my paper to me. "All right, Miss Dixon, we will hear from you now."

I smiled at him as I took it from his hands. I noticed that there was no grade on it, but I didn't think much about that. I looked up at the class, smiling so hard my cheeks hurt. I looked at Nat. He raised his fist halfway and mouthed the words "Way to go, Dianne!" to me. I was enjoying this.

I began reading my story to the class. It was about my genius twins. I had given them telepathic powers, but only between each other. They had discovered a cure for cancer from their experiments with black-eyed peas. One of the girls was kidnapped by the owners of a large drug company, who tried to force her to hand over the cancer cure. They wanted to develop an expensive pharmaceutical from the natural black-eyed peas cure so that they could make a lot of money. But the girls outsmarted the kidnappers. They sent telepathic messages to each other so that the police had no trouble finding the kidnappers' hideout. At the end of the story, I had the twins broadcast their experiments on the news so that everyone would know what the cure was and no drug company would be able to cheat people out of it.

When I finished reading my story, I looked up to see the expressions on the other kids' faces. They were smiling. And then they did something that I never would have expected. They began to clap. They were actually clapping for my story! All except Nancy Cicero, of course.

I looked at Nat and watched him put two fingers in his mouth and whistle, loud. Then I turned my head to look at Mr. Perlman. I wanted to see the face that I usually tried to avoid. I wanted to see what those thin lips looked like when they formed a smile. He stood glaring at me with his hands on his hips and his head tilted to one side. He was squinting his tiny blue eyes, and his lips were pinched tightly together. He cleared his throat and then he spoke.

"Well, well, well, Dianne. That was quite some story. Yes, a very good story in fact. And, as you can see, the whole class enjoyed it. They even clapped for you. So perhaps you will tell us who the author is so that we can give him or her proper credit."

At first I couldn't stop blinking my eyes, as though opening and closing them could somehow change what I had just heard. I was sure I had misunderstood.

"You heard me. We're all waiting. Whose book did you copy that story from? I know you couldn't have written that yourself."

I began to shake. I felt cold. My stomach churned and I half hoped I would vomit . . . yeah, vomit right in Mr. Perlman's face.

I was holding my story in my hand at my side, and slowly I began to crumple it between my fingers, rolling it against my thigh until all six pages were nothing more than a huge ball in my clenched fist.

I looked around the classroom. I could tell from my classmates' expressions that they all believed I had copied my story out of a book. Nancy Cicero was looking smug, as if to say, "I knew you couldn't have written it."

I looked at Nat. He was mad. He was clutching the edge of his desk and staring at Mr. Perlman. I turned back to Mr. Perlman and let out all my feelings of anger and frustration.

"I wrote this story myself," I said through clenched teeth, softly at first. I was not even sure I had spoken.

Mr. Perlman smiled. "Excuse me, Dianne, you said something?"

"I said I wrote this story myself!" I was yelling. I couldn't hold it in. I struggled to keep from crying in shame and embarrassment. I refused to give him that.

"That's right, Mr. Perlman . . . me, I wrote this. I know why that's so hard for you to believe, but that's your problem. I bet if I showed you all the drafts and rewriting I went through to get to this story, you still wouldn't be satisfied, would you, Mr. Perlman? Do you want to ask my mother who wrote this, huh? Would you like to ask both my parents about this? I'll tell them to come here and see you. In fact, I want them to come. I think it's time they talked to you—and maybe the principal too—about the way you treat me and Nat. Is that what you want?"

The room was silent. Mr. Perlman's mouth hung open, but he recovered quickly.

"There's no need to speak with your parents or anybody else's. Evidently the homework assignment I gave you and Nathaniel to do after the last writing assignment paid off. You see that, class? It is possible to improve your writing by paying attention to the . . . ah . . . instructions in your texts. If Dianne can improve her writing, anyone can. Thank you, Dianne. You may take your seat now."

I didn't move.

Mr. Perlman glared at me, folding his arms across his chest.

"I said you may sit down, Dianne. We've heard quite enough from you for one day."

I didn't move.

"What are you waiting for, a handwritten invitation?" Mr. Perlman appeared nervous.

"No," I said. "I'm waiting for my grade. You didn't give me a grade for my story."

I walked over to him and shoved the ball of paper into his hands. He just looked at it at first, and then he looked at me. Slowly, he unwrapped the ball, smoothing out the pages. He walked over to his desk to pick up a pen. He reached out his hand for the red one and then stopped. He glanced back at me and then at the class, pausing for only a moment to look at Nat. He quickly picked up his blue ballpoint pen and scribbled across the top of my paper. Then he shoved the pages back into my hand, a sneer forming at the corners of his mouth.

I took back the pages and walked slowly to my seat. Sitting down next to Nancy, I spread my story out on my desk. I looked at the mark, not quite sure what to feel, until I caught her expression. Then I smiled as I watched her quickly turn her head so as not to see the A- just above the title.

I can still see her now . . . Mr. Perlman too. And I have often wondered how much of my experience in that sixth-grade class has shaped the person I have become. I suppose some credit must be due to Mr. Perlman for my decision to become a civil rights lawyer, a published writer of both fiction and nonfiction, and a teacher of legal writing. Perhaps, then, I have learned that even the most negative of circumstances can yield positive consequences. But he deserves much more "credit" than that, for I have also learned to be deeply suspicious of an entire group of people, based solely on their skin color. In the end, that is a lesson no eleven-year-old, or anyone else for that matter, should ever have to learn.

Anthony Ross

Anthony Ross is a prisoner on death row in San Quentin. "Whether or not I live another second," he says, "I have to reach beyond these prison walls and show someone, anyone, that even in the face of the worst circumstances, anything is possible if you have faith in what you're doing and confidence in yourself."

Anthony began writing in 1989. Completely self-taught, he says that as a writer he is constantly developing, constantly trying to take his work to the next level. "I write to connect with others, with the creative energy inside and beyond me, and, ultimately, with myself." In 1995 Anthony's short story "Walker's Requiem" received a PEN award.

In the story that follows, Anthony recounts two horrific experiences with racism that he says caused him to hate white people so much that, for the first time in his life, he considered killing them. "I hope the reader is able to understand how single events and choices can have cosmic effects," he says. "I went on to drop out of school a couple of years later, and I became a gang member. I've been in prison for seventeen years."

A few words of Anthony Ross's story have been omitted so that it could be included in this young adult edition.

LITTLE TIGERS DON'T ROAR

On a May day in Los Angeles, in 1970, when I was eleven years old, two things happened that changed my life.

I had taken to riding the RTD bus down to the Black Panthers' small storefront office on Broadway. The walls of the reception area were covered with posters of Huey Newton sitting in a wicker chair; a rifle, a spear, the eyes of a cat, and "Free Huey" flyers were stacked all around the office. Behind the desk a huge flag hung on the wall with a black panther on it that looked like it was ready to leap.

For a few hours after school each day, I ran errands, passed out flyers, and listened to a beautiful sister with a big Afro rap about some guy named Mao as she read from a little red book she claimed would fix everything. (She sure had me convinced.) Afterward, they would let the kids who'd helped out that day eat all the cookies and doughnuts we wanted.

On the day that Huey Newton was to be released from prison, I took a stand of my own at

West Athens Elementary School. My teacher, a fiftyish white woman named Mrs. Paget, had just called me a nigger because I refused to stay in the classroom while she read *Little Black Sambo* aloud to the class. There was something about that story that made me angry, something in the way Mrs. Paget read it that gave me the distinct feeling that Sambo was in the classroom and she fully expected him to come forward holding a big plate of flapjacks.

"Don't be a nigger, Ross," she said as I walked out of the classroom.

It was my first real experience with the issue of race, and her words made me conscious of my blackness in a way that all of the black power and black pride slogans down at the Panther office had not. This was the first of two things that happened that day that changed my life.

When . . . why . . . how . . . did I become a nigger? The questions exploded in my mind. It had never occurred to me that, even though I was one of the best students in her class, to her I still was, at the core, a nigger. The word was hurled with all the force of slavery behind it, and it stung just as deeply as if I'd been hit with a bullwhip.

That afternoon I hooked up with a cat I hung out with named Billy Cadwell. He ran it down to me about Huey being freed. "He's outta jail, man, and there's gonna be some righteous [expletive] going down now!" Billy, who was also eleven, considered us Black Panthers. He'd stolen us each a black tam from the New York Hat Store in downtown Los Angeles, saying, "All we gotta do now is get us some leather coats."

But I knew it meant more than that. I told him, "Naw, man, we gotta meet Mao first," remembering what the sister had said, knowing there was a connection somewhere. "Then we meet Huey and help fix things in the ghetto."

"Right on," Billy said, holding up a clenched fist.

I told Billy I wanted to go down to the Panther office but didn't have money for the bus.

"I'm tapped too, man," he said, pulling out his pockets for emphasis.

After giving our situation some thought, we decided to go try to collect some golf balls for some quick change at the golf course in Gardena, a small suburb on the south end of Los Angeles that was predominately white and Asian with just a smidgen of blacks. I rode all the way there on the handlebars of Billy's Schwinn bike, but when we got there the place was closing.

"Now what we gonna do, Tony?" Billy asked as we stood in front of the golf course contemplating our next move.

"I'll think of something," I said. But I didn't have a clue as to what we were going to do. And that's when the second thing happened that changed my life.

A white kid about our age walked up to us. "Hey, you guys aren't supposed to be here. You better leave." His voice carried that same tone I'd heard in Mrs. Paget's voice. The same tone as the white manager at Ralph's supermarket used when he asked, "You here to buy something?" It was a tone that came down from some high peak I was never supposed to ascend, a tone that pushed without apology.

"Well?" the white kid asked, his bright blue eyes embodying both problem and solution.

I socked him so fast it made Billy flinch. I told the kid to give me all his money. Stunned, he reached into his pocket and took out a few bills. I snatched them, feeling a heightened sense of his whiteness—my blackness. I hopped on the handlebars, and Billy took off like a demon was on our heels.

"Man, you decked that [expletive] white boy!" Billy shouted in my ear, laughing.

But I wasn't laughing. I wasn't even thinking about that white kid any longer. I was thinking about whether or not I would go back to school ever again.

We made it to Helen Keller Park, about a mile away. A dark ring of sweat was working its way around Billy's collar. "Tony, you gonna have to go to the office without me," Billy said, holding his stomach and breathing hard.

"Why?" I asked, thinking something might be wrong with his health.

" 'Cause," he grimaced, "I gotta dookie reeeal bad."

We both laughed. "It's cool, man. I'll tell you all about it when I get back."

We gave each other a soul handshake, and then

Billy sped off for home, hunched down over the handlebars, feet pumping the pedals at a dizzying speed.

I began walking up Vermont Avenue toward the bus stop, but I didn't get two blocks before I heard the sudden wail of a siren that made me turn around to see a police car speeding toward me with lights flashing. It jumped the curb and came to a halt, inches from my legs. I stepped back, ready to bolt, when two white sheriffs hopped out, guns drawn, screaming at the top of their lungs. "Lay down, [expletive]! Get on the [expletive] ground."

I stood frozen, unable to move. "You better lay down, [expletive]!" they screamed. I wanted to—God knows I wanted to—but my brain was short-circuited. I was scared [expletive]. From somewhere behind me I heard voices pleading for me to lie down. Someone—a woman—begged, "Please, son, don't give them a reason to kill you."

Kill me? The words spun in my mind like an out-of-control Disney ride. I heard a childlike voice ask, "What'd I do?" I didn't even realize it was my own voice until one of the sheriffs yelled, "You're under arrest for robbery."

The entire scene switched to slow motion. "On the ground, [expletive], or I will blow your [expletive] head off!" he screamed, each word dripping with venom. I knew instinctively that he would kill me.

Taking that kid's money still hadn't registered, but I did finally get my motor skills to work and

I lay on the ground. The men rushed over and I felt a knee come down hard on my neck, knocking my face into the pavement and busting my lip. They pulled my arms back, sending a shock wave of pain through my shoulders. One of them handcuffed me, and the other one knocked the tam from my head and whispered, "Another second and I'd blow you away . . . you hear me, nigger?"

I said nothing.

The two of them yanked me up off the ground, and a fresh bolt of pain shot through my shoulders. They hauled me to the police car, where I saw the moon face of the white kid looking tearfully out at me from the backseat. My heart pounded in my chest. This wasn't about the money anymore. It was about an old equation of black and white, about place and status. Again, something instinctive gripped me as I stood there, my black skin seeming to take on some awful substance that separated me from everything, making me conscious of who I was, who I was not—a substance that saddled me with a deep hatred for myself, for whites. I had no idea of what it was like to be black in America, but I knew what it was like being black in Los Angeles.

"This the one?" one of the sheriffs asked the white kid.

I prayed the kid had lost his memory. No such luck—he nodded his head, mumbling, "Uh-huh."

I felt like a gigantic fist had knocked me down,

and for a moment I was overcome with the sensation of vertigo. I was falling . . . falling into the racial quicksand with no way out.

The sheriffs got the money from me, gave it to the kid, and told him to go home. They tossed me into the backseat, where I bounced on the handcuffs, immediately tightening them. I asked if they could loosen them, and my question was met with a barrage of obscenities. I was told to shut my [expletive] mouth or my nigger ass would be put in the trunk.

As we drove away, I saw the sidewalk was lined with people, black people. Their faces showed not the slightest hint of protest or concern. Instead, I saw a mixture of fear and relief. I wished the Panthers were there. I wished Huey was there.

The two sheriffs apparently found delight in my pain, and they intentionally drove over every pothole, bump, and manhole cover they could find en route to the Lennox Sheriff Station. The sheriff on the passenger side would point and say, "Look, look, here comes another one." And then they would burst out laughing when I winced from the cuffs biting into my wrists. For the entire ride, I had to endure the steady onslaught of profanity, threats, and laughter as they described in detail how they were going to kill me and then dump my body in a vacant lot or behind a trash dumpster.

"Just another dead nigger," the sheriff who was driving said.

"Yeah, who's gonna care about that?" asked the sheriff on the passenger side, turning to me.

I sat in my own silence, trying to escape the inescapable. And as if he could read my mind, the sheriff on the passenger side asked, "What you thinking about, nigger, you wanna escape, huh?" He looked over at the driver and yelled, "Stop the car! The nigger is trying to escape."

His partner hit the brakes. My head whiplashed, hitting the back of the front seat. They both drew their guns, pointing them at my head. I shut my eyes, crunched my small frame into the seat, and waited to be shot. But no shot came—just the loud yell of "Boom!" making me jump. I opened my eyes. The two sheriffs were cracking up.

All that I had ever heard about police was confirmed by these two, so once we arrived at the substation and I was pulled from the backseat, I tried to make a run for it. I got almost a full two feet before one of them snatched my shirt collar, swung me around, and sank his fist in my stomach. I folded up into a ball of pain, trying to suck in gulps of air as they dragged me across the ground toward a brick building.

"What you got there?" someone asked.

"A little monkey," one of the sheriffs answered.

"Come on, we got a nice cage for him," a voice said.

I heard the jingling of keys as they pulled me down a dimly lit hallway with large steel doors on the sides. Someone shouted from behind one of the doors, "Do me like that, you punk pig!"

The men paid no attention to the challenge as they half kicked, half threw me into a small dank cell.

I could see the sheriff with the keys. On the shoulder of his shirt were yellow stripes. "What this one do?" he asked.

"Robbed a little white kid," the sheriff who'd driven us there told him.

"The nigger also tried to run on us, Sergeant," the other sheriff added, smiling.

The sergeant leaned over me and said, "Boy, we gon teach you bout messin wit our kind."

They started hitting and kicking my whole body. Every ounce of emotion I had was being beat out of me. A seething hatred would be the only thing left.

I hadn't realized they had stopped until I heard the steel door slam shut. I glanced up from the floor and saw a pale face peering through a small window in the center of the door. "You better get used to it, nigger. You just better get used to it."

I felt, rather than thought, that this is how things are, but I was angry and I needed to protest. I rose from the floor and started banging on the door, screaming. "Come back, [expletive]! I'll kill you! You pigs! Honky [expletive]!" I kept it up for about ten minutes—until older and stronger voices from the other cells joined in, drowning me out. I lay on the steel cot, my body bruised, numb. Eventually I fell asleep out of exhaustion . . . and rage.

Sometime later I awoke to the sound of jingling keys and the door opened. I had lost all sense of time, and it seemed as if I had been in the cell for a day or two; actually, it had only been a few hours. In the doorway stood a white man wearing a suit. We stared at each other for a moment, and finally he said, "If you ever come back, I'ma kick your black ass personally."

He took me out into a lighted reception room, where my mother sat on a long wooden bench. I could see she had been crying.

"What them people do to you?" Mamma asked me in the car.

For some reason I didn't tell her. Maybe I thought there was nothing she could do, that it was too late. All I could think about for days afterward was how I wanted to kill a white policeman. In the span of a few hours I had gone from an eleven-year-old who made one mistake to one with enough racial hatred to kill. And, before that day, I had never thought about killing anyone.

That night I told Mamma about Mrs. Paget, and the next morning she marched into the principal's office demanding that something be done. The school took immediate action—they merely transferred me out of Mrs. Paget's class into another one. And she just kept right on teaching and reading that Black Sambo book.

As I grew up, my life became so inextricably bound up in black and white that, no matter where I went, I couldn't avoid seeing things in those terms. I searched for confrontation, perhaps even creating it at times. The race [crap] was always there, soiling and dominating everything I did. It was an insane way to grow up, an insane way to live. And just as the two white sheriffs had zealously threatened, I was killed that day . . . my boyhood buried beneath the harsh, often violent, reality of race.

Aya de León

———◆———

Aya de León grew up feeling racially displaced and alienated, severed from both her African-American and Puerto Rican roots. Now in her early thirties, she lives in the Oakland Bay area of California, in an artists' compound with other women of color.

"This was a difficult story to write," Aya says, "because it required me to go back to the emotional reality of childhood. I had to remember the isolation and mutual mistrust of black people as well as the devastation of my relationship with my father. In my adult life, I have worked hard to be a good sister in the black community, to be emotionally and spiritually grounded, and to be politically clear. But this story from my childhood reflects a time of confusion, disorientation, and buried grief."

The author of several stories and articles, Aya says she sees herself as a political and spiritual writer. "I write about race, class, and gender," she says. "I write about black people and emotional and spiritual transformation." When she is not writing, she works as the coordinator of an alcohol and drug treatment program for teens and as the director of the Mothertongue Institute for Creative Development in Oakland, which provides classes and workshops in the Bay Area and beyond.

HITTING DANTE

I suspect it was a big, bad sixth-grader who first came up to me talking about my mama. I can imagine the scene: this sixth-grader marching up to me on the Franklin Elementary School playground and getting in my face. And I was thinking, *How does she know my mother? Did she see my mom pick me up after school? Did my mom come down here one time and I didn't know about it?*

Despite a palpitation of terror in my solar plexus, I blinked at her several times and let my eyes slide down to the asphalt. As I focused on the ground, I saw a silver pull tab from a soda can glinting from beneath the toe of my purple high-top Converse All-Star sneakers.

"Did you hear me?" she demanded. "I said 'I saw your mama on the ho' stro' last night.' "

"Tiffany, leave that girl alone!" the yard teacher said. She was a black woman in her forties with brassy red hair.

Eyes on the ground, I stooped to pick up the pull tab. I didn't see Tiffany suck her teeth and

101

stalk off or the yard teacher walk away, shaking her head in pity for me.

I tore off the sharp silver tongue of the pull tab and put the ring on my finger. *I am the princess with a jewel from my father, the king; I am a space explorer and the ring is my walkie-talkie to my ship; I am a gypsy and my ring will ward off all evil.*

It wasn't what the girl said that was so terrible; it was that she said it and *waited*. She stood there, fists on her bony hips, socks accusingly crisp and white, each of her braids so perfectly contained. She was *waiting* for me to respond. I was a black girl, wasn't I? I was supposed to know what a ho' stro' was, or at least get the gist of it and ready up to defend my mama's honor. I was supposed to have a black mama at home—not a blond Puerto Rican mom—who would take me in her arms and say, *Don't cry, my little dumpling. It doesn't matter what that girl said about me. That girl doesn't even know me.*

It would have been different if I had grown up in New York or Miami and there had been some other way to be black. Some *café con leche* way to be black, some *oye, mamita* way to be black. But I grew up in Berkeley, California, and the only way to be black was about greens and cornbread, and I didn't know anything about that. My father was black, was even a blues musician. But he was on the road, sharing African-American culture with the world, leaving me at home to fend for myself.

My Latina mother and white stepfather could

comfort me in my troubling run-ins with black kids, but they couldn't translate for me: *That girl is trying to engage you, is testing you, singling you out. There may even be a timid offer of friendship peeking out from under that barbed-wire exterior.*

It is easy to long for New York, or some kind of Puerto Ricanness, but only in Berkeley could I be so soft and get all the way through public school without getting beat up. Except for that one time I hit Dante.

In Berkeley schools in the 1970s, black kids mostly left me alone to play with my two best friends, Anne and Emily, who were white and Asian. While the black girls played hopscotch or jump rope, my friends and I played elaborate serial make-believe games at recess.

Throughout grade school, I watched the black kids with a bewildered fascination. I watched them timidly, for fear of being noticed even in my watching: *What you lookin' at?* Real black kids always had a snappy comeback. They could fight, play kickball, and never let you see them cry. I came to school with a lumpy natural and ashy caramel-colored knees, but real black kids came to school, skin in all shades of brown, shiny with Vaseline. Girls started the day with scalps smarting from sharp combs that parted even rows for braids. Boys had piks peeking out of the back pockets of their Toughskins jeans to keep their Afros round. Real black kids were named Shawnelle, LeMar, and DelTrina. Dante was a real black kid.

Dante had been in my class since fourth grade. He wasn't big and bad like LaVell, whose conked hair stuck straight back and who was always getting sent to the office. Dante was short and wiry with crooked front teeth and a rusty brown Afro that matched his skin. I was bigger than Dante and probably the same brown.

Dante didn't look for trouble, but he was sure to laugh extra loud if someone was getting capped on for having shoes from Kmart. I could never understand what was so funny about that.

Dante and the other black boys in my class always played kickball or dodgeball during lunch and recess. During p.e., the teacher would usually let us do what we wanted, as long as we kept moving. My friends and I would pretend to be archaeologists, hunting the playground's asphalt for Moroccan brown diamonds, which looked suspiciously like fragments of beer bottles.

Sometimes the p.e. teacher would make the whole class play kickball. Once, when Dante was captain, he picked me last. This was usual, but he didn't want to have me on the team at all. He groaned out loud when I was up to kick and Marcus, captain of the other team, clapped his hands together, grinning and yelling, "Easy out! Easy out!"

I would step up timidly to kick, ready to get it over with so Marcus would shut up. Sometimes I made it to first base and even made it home.

After I was up, I ignored the game, doing handstands up against the chain-link fence. When the other team was up, I would brush the gravel from my palms and head outfield. "Way out," Dante would say, because everyone knew I couldn't catch. I practiced cartwheels, and the ball rarely came my way. When it did, I would just duck and cover my head, hearing the red rubber bounce savagely off the ground just behind me.

I ducked from the ball; I shrank from confrontations. What could have possessed me to hit this boy? Dante and I weren't friends, weren't enemies. Not before or after I hit him. It was no big deal to him. He probably tousled with siblings or cousins on a regular basis. But I, the only child in the lost tribe of my family, was breaking new ground with my violence.

What pushed me over the line?

Twenty years later I am searching for an answer. I round up the usual suspects and dismiss them all. I didn't want the teacher's attention—she was out of the room. I didn't have a crush on him. I wasn't showing off. It wasn't self-defense either—I *initiated* the fight with him. The violence is so clear, but my underlying ten-year-old reasons are silent, absent, hidden.

Slowly, a hypothesis crystallizes. I will never be able to prove it, but a new suspect emerges. A new conjecture makes the pieces fit together. I go back and fill in the empty space. I can't vouch for all the details—even some of the names have been changed—but the heart is true.

I woke up at seven forty-five that morning with KFRC, a Top 40 radio station, on my beige plastic radio. It had a dial clock on one side and a beige-and-gold speaker on the other. I listened to Air Supply's "Lost in Love" as I lay under the soft blue cotton comforter with the faux patchwork pattern.

By the time I came downstairs, my stepfather had already gone to work at the restaurant he owned. My mom baked the desserts for his restaurant, and she was sitting at the big wooden kitchen table frosting a lemon tart in a crisscross pattern with meringue.

I noticed six other tarts cooling on the counter and ready to be frosted. I got my breakfast cereal and set the heavy half gallon of milk down next to my bowl.

My mom looked up. "Don't bump the table!" she snapped.

I froze, then went back to preparing my cereal in slow motion, pretending I was bionic, like when they showed Lindsay Wagner running real slow. I kept my eyes on my mom, who tucked a strand of straight, dark blond hair behind her ear as she went back to work. Her hair was naturally a sandy brown that teetered on the edge of blondness. Sometimes she sprayed Sun-In on it to make it blonder.

As I ate my cereal, my eyes traveled idly over the piles of paper on the table: an *Oakland Tribune* from the day before, the previous Sunday's *San Francisco Chronicle*. That's when I saw him. Peeking out from underneath last Sunday's full-color comics that I'd already read, in the pink section, where they had the movie guy with the pointy nose and the hat who jumped out of his chair and clapped for reasons I didn't understand.

It was an ad for Jordan Rivers in concert in San Francisco the weekend before. It was Wednesday. He was my father.

He was smiling impersonally up at me, and I felt an incredible amount of something and nothing at the same time. Like I got all ready to feel something, then changed my mind.

He was here, or had been here, and hadn't called—again. I did not answer a knock at the door to find his towering presence. To me, he was a giant. Big arms, big hands, big feet. He was more of an event than a person. He was a dark pumpernickel brown, with my same small, slanted eyes, but his nose was flatter and his nostrils wider. I was getting to be tall like him, and my feet were already too big for kids' shoes. When he did visit it was usually unexpected, and I was always shy around him. I was likely to say a quiet, startled "Daddy?" before he embraced me with a loud, gravelly "Hey, baby."

I slid the comics all the way over the pink section, over the ad. Then I moved my bowl around in slow circles, making the cereal into a whirlpool.

"I told you not to bump the table, goddamit!" my mom yelled.

I cringed. "Sorry." Not hungry, I took the bowl, fished the soggy cereal into the garbage, and dumped the milk in the sink.

When I looked up at the clock, it was only two minutes till my bus would leave.

"Bye, Mom, I'm late."

She looked up, not really mad, just tired. "Bye, dear."

I didn't have time to kiss her before I grabbed my Day-Glo orange pack and ran down the red wooden steps and up the block for the bus.

I just made it that day, and I slumped into the green vinyl seat, winded and distracted, as the bus pulled off. Dante didn't ride my bus or live in my neighborhood. I didn't know where he lived. Maybe he came to school that day with his own baggage, his own readiness to snap.

Marcus had Jolly Rancher candies that day. I sat in front of him and I could smell the watermelon and green apple flavors. Dante and LaVell noticed too, and kept looking over at him.

We were learning about Japanese-American history. "During World War II, I felt really ashamed to be Japanese," Ms. Yamada was telling the class. "People said, 'Oh, those sneaky Japanese.' I tried to act super-American to let people know I wasn't the enemy."

LaVell raised his hand: "Ms. Yamada, can I go to the bathroom?"

I bet he just wants to get some candy.

"Okay, LaVell. But I want you back in five minutes."

LaVell jumped up from his desk and went to get the cardboard bathroom pass. He sidled up to Marcus on his way out the door, and Marcus passed him a Jolly Rancher. *See, I knew he was faking.*

Ms. Yamada's back was turned as she wrote vocabulary words on the board.

seize
internment

Dante put his hands up for Marcus to throw him a Jolly Rancher. Marcus looked at the teacher, turned to Dante, and shook his head no. Dante sucked his teeth in disappointment. *God, they bug me. Why can't they just pay attention?*

Ms. Yamada turned from the board. "Emily, will you see if there's any chalk on my desk?"

Emily crossed the room. The chalk in Ms. Yamada's hand had become tiny—the size of a jelly bean.

Emily looked on the desktop. "I don't see any."

Ms. Yamada walked over to her desk. "Thanks anyway, Emily."

As Emily went back to her seat and Ms. Yamada rummaged through her desk for chalk, Dante said, "Come on, man," in an urgent whisper. *Shut up, Dante. He's not gonna give you any.*

Ms. Yamada looked up. "You guys should be copying down the vocabulary words." *Yeah. Be quiet and do your work.* She kept opening and closing drawers. Dante lowered his head as if to copy the board, then turned to Marcus. "Come on," he mouthed. *Why are boys so dumb?* Ms. Yamada was kneeling in front of her desk, head obscured. Dante put his hands up again. Marcus considered it, looked at the teacher, and prepared to throw.

"I can't find any chalk," Ms. Yamada said. "Listen you guys, finish copying down those words. I'll be back in one minute."

She left the door open, but the moment she stepped out, Dante popped up from his desk and came over to Marcus with his hand out. *I hope she comes back and catches them.*

"Ugh, I don't like watermelon. You got anything else? Apple! Yeah, yeah! Aw, nigga, gimme more than one!"

"I ain't got that many." *Why don't they just shut up?* I poked my pencil into a groove in the desk and the lead broke.

"Come on, Marcus . . ." Dante whined.

Marcus gave Dante a second piece as I stood up to sharpen my pencil. Dante turned to head back to his desk. We collided.

"Ugh, Aya, watch where you're going!"

And suddenly something in my brain told something in my arm to propel my hand through the space between us. I hit him. I smacked him hard in the shoulder.

I didn't even see his face react, his focus sharpen, his lips contract into a tight circle. I just felt the blow, the thundering shove in my chest, and then the floor as it leapt up to catch me.

Dante stalked back to his desk. No one said anything. I lay dazed for a second on the olive-green carpet. There were staples and tiny fragments of paper caught in the dark loops that the custodian's weekly vacuuming didn't pick up.

As I stood up on unsteady legs and slid back

into my desk chair, my numbness disintegrated. I barely had time to put my head down before the tears descended, hot and involuntary.

Ms. Yamada came back with LaVell in tow. LaVell lingered by Marcus's desk on his way to his own.

"Have a seat, LaVell," Ms. Yamada said, her eyes following him until he did so.

She scanned the room from behind her thick, round glasses. We were all in our seats. It didn't occur to her to look at me. I never fought, never got in trouble. I turned my work in on time, got good grades, rarely talked in class when I wasn't supposed to.

She took her new, full-length piece of chalk and finished writing the vocabulary words on the board:

seize
internment
reparations

She did not notice me with my head down. No one told. My only fight got to be my private defeat in the world of my classmates. I cried in embarrassment and pain.

And relief. And gratitude. Tears spilled out from underneath Dante's handprint on my chest. All of the shame that had been patiently waiting could be released. Tears spilled out and across my folded brown arms. I could feel worthless. Tears ran down the beige fake wood surface of my desk.

I could feel alone. Tears soaked into my navy-blue T-shirt. Several dripped down onto my thighs and dotted the rust-colored fabric of my corduroy bell-bottoms. I could feel utterly desolate. Tears spilled out because no one had taught me, forced me, to bottle up like real black kids. I could feel lacerated and incomplete.

Tears spilled out until I was empty and could wipe my eyes and nose with the soft cotton fabric of my T-shirt. *Thank God I have something to cry about, instead of my stupid dad who I don't even care about anyway.* Tears spilled out until I could pick my head back up and pay attention to the teacher. By the time I looked up, the edge of the chalk was rounded.

> seize—to grab something
> internment—to be locked up
> reparation—

Dante was engrossed in drawing a picture on the brown paper bag cover of his math book. Marcus was sneaking a Jolly Rancher candy into his mouth. Anne and Emily were copying down what the teacher had written. LaVell was going to get a check mark by his name on the board because he was interrupting the teacher, hissing at Marcus to give him another piece of candy.

I stood up to sharpen my pencil.

Antoine P. Reddick

———◆———

In his early forties and living in New Haven, Connecticut, Antoine Reddick says his "first and only story" is a tribute to all the members of his family who died young, struggling with racism, poverty, and crime.

ALL THE BLACK CHILDREN

Sixteen children is a very large family, and I was number ten. I was raised in New Haven, Connecticut, a college town of predominantly middle-class liberal whites, in the 1960s. It was a time of civil unrest: the Vietnam war was headline news and desegregation was being pushed and fought for in the streets all over the country. But these events had no effect on me or my family at that time.

To raise sixteen children costs a lot of money, and it was beyond my mother and father's abilities. Since my father had no kind of useful education and was unskilled, my mother went to the state for help. She had to declare my father as missing or delinquent in his role as a parent. She had no choice, there was no other way to support so many children.

My father became the outcast of the family. Legally, he could not live with us or he would have to pay child support. If he didn't pay, he would go to jail.

I'm not sure when my father became an alcoholic or what the cause of his heavy drinking was, but it started before I was born. As I grew older I hardly saw him except when he would come by to beg money from Mother for drinking. My mother loved my father, but drinking became his life, and we children could not be part of his love and affection anymore. He became a stranger to us.

The result was that my mother was left with a houseful of kids, dependent on welfare. I should have been grateful that we lived in a house. Most black families on welfare lived in a low-income housing project on the other side of town. Even with four bedrooms, though, there was not enough space for us to live comfortably. My sisters had their room, and the older boys theirs, but we smaller children had to find space where we could. Five of us slept in the same bed, which seemed normal to me.

At that time, the nation was caught up in busing black children to desegregated schools. I and a few of my brothers and sisters were bused to a school in the suburbs with all white students. And most of the teachers were white as well. I was the only black kid in the classroom, but I felt equal. I made friends, I played with the white children, and they invited me to their homes.

A Jewish kid named Jeff Novak became a close friend, and I would spend the night at his home. It was hard to believe that such a small family (he, his mother, his father, and his younger brother) could live in such a big house all by themselves. They had two cars and lived in a beautiful neighborhood with clean streets and cut lawns. Jeff's father was a doctor, so we rarely saw him. His mother was a nice woman who would drive us to the movies or to the park. They ate dinner together as a family, which was new to me because at my house food was not plentiful—when it was there at all.

I was accepted by these white people for reasons I did not question, even though my clothes were hand-me-downs or secondhand. They never stopped me from being part of their world.

But when I left their big house and Jeff's mother would drop me off at home in their shiny new car and drive away, the dream would come to a halt. I was back to a world and a life that I began to hate. There were no cars, no toys, no bikes. There was never enough food, money, clothes, or even love. My mother could only focus her attention on the babies she still had to raise. I know she loved us all the best she could, but being a single parent was hard on my mother. With every bit of her endurance she held us together as a family, but the struggle was hopeless.

My older brothers and sister found escape in the streets. There they could forget the poverty and destitution of living in an overcrowded house. The streets were a new way to survive as black children. With no father to guide us and no discipline, as a family we became totally dysfunctional.

Drugs were a big part of the struggle for change in the 1960s. And drugs became the answer to a lot of problems—or so most kids thought. My brothers and sister found their dreams in the drug houses and back alleys, where narcotics ran free and were easy to buy or sell. It would be years before I realized the destructive effect drugs would have on my family and my life. They turned into a fire that spread through my family and dominated our lives.

With the drugs, came crime. As a child, I had no understanding of crime or drugs, but many nights the police visited our house, asking for one or the other of my brothers. Some crime had been committed, and they were involved. It was a strange and scary feeling to be awakened in the middle of the night by big white men with flashlights searching the house from top to bottom, looking for my brothers.

My mother always protected them and denied they were about. After the police left, my mother and sisters would sit and talk in low voices, feeling bewildered and helpless. But the drugs and crime would go on for years to come—shooting drugs in the house, bringing home stolen property, coming and going at all hours of the night and day. My mother was helpless to act. She had five sons who were too old and too big to send to their rooms for discipline. All she could do was pray.

My mother never gave up on us younger children. She pushed us to go to school, and she enrolled us in summer camp programs. Camp was the best time of my childhood. For two weeks

I was free of my poverty and free to be a kid. Getting on that bus, heading for the campground, was so thrilling and new. Getting out of the city and into the woods still touches me today as an experience of wonder and joy. Being with other kids, sleeping in cabins, swimming, and sitting around the campfire singing—I felt like a part of something. Camp showed me that the world was not all fear and hate, that it could be a place of peace and a newborn joy. I was not poor or black any longer, I was just a kid with a heart full of excitement and adventure.

But the dream always came to an end when I returned home. Nothing had changed. My family still had to struggle from day to day, for money was everybody's urgency. Economics played such a dominating role in my family's life and mine.

I began to ask why my family never seemed to have the kind of life the white families enjoyed. I loved my family very much and, struggling along with them, I accepted the poverty and the slums in which I lived, but secretly, inside me, I yearned to live like the white children. The color of their skin meant happiness. I wanted to spend my life at summer camp and stay over at the white children's homes and be a part of their world. But it was a world I would never know because my skin was black, and poverty ruled my life. I thought there would never be a chance for me as long as my skin was black.

Slowly I began to notice the difference between being black and poor and living in a crowded run-down house and being white and living in a nice home in a clean neighborhood. In my heart and mind, frustration began to form along with hate for these separate societies.

The awareness of bigotry, discrimination, and segregation came into my life. Crime was the way I struck out at all of this; it became the most destructive force in my life.

I had plenty of teachers to lead me into this life of crime. One who stands out is my brother Eddie, who is five years older than me. I looked up to him as most kids do their big brothers. In my eyes he was a hero who feared nothing, knew everything, and lived the way he chose. He dressed well, had girlfriends, and drove cars. He had a charm about him that drew me in but ended up being totally detrimental to me for the rest of my life.

My brother was a breed apart from the rest of my family. He looked down on my brothers and sisters who did drugs or drank alcohol. He believed himself to be smarter than anyone else, and I believed in him. But what he taught me was a form of deterioration and destruction that slowly chipped away at any chance of my having a morally or ethically decent and honest life.

Today they would call my brother a player or hustler—a smooth-talking, confident liar. He was without love or feelings for anyone but himself, and shame never crossed his mind about the way he used family and friends.

Naive, gullible, and young, I was the perfect

person for him to use and abuse. I was elated to join him in his life of crime. I was fourteen years old, wanting excitement and adventure. I could have found it in sports, fishing, camping—or even a good job—if someone would have pointed me in the right direction. The cost of following Eddie's influence was a high price to pay. Twenty-five years later, I'm still paying the cost of learning from him about crime.

At the time, I believed in my brother and I wanted to prove myself to him. He would wake me in the middle of the night to go on these unknown missions—stealing cars, burglarizing, and committing other crimes. The money and property we stole had no great meaning to me; it was the excitement of it that filled my childish mind. One night we were caught and charged with burglary. My brother, being older, was sent to jail, and I was sent to the juvenile center. It would be years before I would ever see my brother again. Since I was a minor, the juvenile court gave me six months in a boys' school thirty miles from home.

I look back on these events wanting to hate my brother for the seeds of destruction he planted in my head. But it goes deeper than my brother— poverty, drugs, unemployment, and discrimination all play a part. My brother's ideas were all wrong and damaging to me as a child, but poverty, frustration, and hate for a society that refused black children equality as human beings were the creators of the crimes we committed.

The boy's school I was sent to was not as bad as

I had feared. There were tough kids and street-smart kids, most of them from broken homes or dysfunctional families, white and black, so I didn't feel alone. My mother visited me when she could. The six months passed, and I came home a little older, but still full of doubts about my life and what the future would bring.

I started junior high school and was bused to a racially mixed school in the suburbs. The kids came from all over town and those who were black were as poverty-stricken as I was but, coming from the projects, they were distinctly different in their attitudes. They were loud, aggressive, and very hostile—attitudes stemming from the environment in which they were raised. They had a grudge against the system and society for having to live in neighborhoods of total destitution. You had to be tough to live in the projects, where the gangs, the drug dealers, drunks, and hustlers all struggled to survive. It wasn't hard for me to understand their dislike for the system and white society. It seemed that nobody cared how they lived or who they were. They lived as outcasts from society.

I was fifteen years old when I made a friend, a boy who lived in the projects named Anthony Redford. I'll never forget the day he invited me home with him. He lived in one of the many high-rise buildings that were in total ruin. The halls were filled with trash, the stairwells smelled of urine, and the walls and doors were spray-painted with graffitti. Most of the apartment doors and windows had been kicked or broken into.

The nighttime was a very dangerous time to walk the streets of this neighborhood. To hear gunfire was common, and cars sped up and down the streets. It was very rare to see police enter these buildings. Only for serious kinds of emergencies would they venture into the dark halls. And white people were never seen in the streets, day or night. They were very much afraid of what hid in the alleys and side streets of these poverty-dominated black environments.

The white people who did venture into this world were usually drug addicts. They came from the suburbs and colleges looking to buy drugs. They always came in quickly, with frightened faces and eager, false smiles, knowing the danger if things went bad, which they sometimes did. They became targets for the rip-off artists and stickup men who lived there—men and women who preyed on anyone they could profit from. Shootings, stabbings, and killings were common.

Summer in the projects was the worst time of year. The smell of the sewers and the trash rotting in the heat on the streets was nauseating. There was no happiness for black children growing up in this environment. These streets were where I learned what being black and welfare-dependent was all about. I forgot about the white kids and their big houses and clean neighborhoods. These were my people, and I belonged with them in the struggle for life and what we could grab or force from a society that gave us nothing to build on, nothing to live for.

The impression that the environment of the projects and the people who lived there left inside me was one of sorrow and pain. I spent years in the project neighborhoods trying to understand why black people were placed so low down in society's system.

I turned eighteen years old, but I felt older from hanging with the rough crowd in the projects. School was my only chance to escape from the mounting chaos. When black history was added to my class schedule, it brought dramatic change to my whole outlook.

For the first time in American history, black children were being taught the origin of their ancestors by professional teachers. My class was taught by a black woman named Ms. Magumba. She dressed in African robes and colorful head wraps. She seemed out of place in this formally dressed society, but she fascinated me. I felt she was part of a culture that was truly born of black people and belonged to us. She seemed very proud to be black, and she said that Africa was a continent as great and wondrous as any nation in the world.

In all the years that I had attended school, nothing touched me more than to learn that black people had been kings and queens of great nations and empires in a world so different from the poverty, crime, and drug-filled streets I walked each day.

I left school my first day that year in bewilderment. It had taken eighteen years for me to learn that there had been and still is a great culture that was part of me and my family. In one word, I finally understood why black men, women, and children struggle to survive. Slavery—it was so hard to accept and understand that black people were bought and sold like cattle and sheep.

It's 1972: Men had walked on the moon, the atom had been split, and science was moving at the speed of light. It seemed unbelievable that just four hundred years earlier, black men, women, and children belonged to white people as property. Slave ships, plantations, and auction blocks were a big part of this nation's history. Black men and women came off the ships in neck chains and leg irons. They were stripped of a culture they would never know again. They were refused education and human rights. I finally saw why the black people of this country had nothing to show but frustration, hatred, and poverty. Black men and women were no more than tools to the whites of that time. Still, four hundred years later, blacks have very little to show for their suffering and the degrading struggle they were forced by the whites to endure.

When school ended for the season, I might have left feeling that what I learned in my black history class was just history—something from the past that could not be changed. But it was not easy to put the subject out of my mind: images of slave ships with black people packed on top of one another, many of them dying from disease and lack of food and fresh water; the whips and chains, and the burning sun beating down on them as they labored endless hours and days in the fields of the plantations.

I'd never thought of myself as a racist or bigot, but it was hard to fight the feeling of hate that slowly grew in me for the white race. I had slept in their houses, played with their children, eaten at their tables, and I was envious of their lives. But I felt tricked and betrayed. These were confusing emotions for me, and that summer I took them into the streets with very destructive results.

The kids I chose to hang out with were a very tough and defiant gang. Crime—getting over on the system—was like a game to them. They talked of the easy money to be made in robbery. A gun was easy to come by in the slums and back alleys of New Haven, and on a hot summer day in July of 1975 I joined a few kids and robbed a store in a white neighborhood.

I was arrested and charged with robbery. I was eighteen years old and locked in a cell with steel bars and no windows. A feeling of total helplessness and misery took hold of me so tight that I wished I were dead. When my mother came to the jail to visit me, I was filled with shame and longing for her to hold me and tell me it would be all right and we could go home. But that would not happen for years. I was given five years in a reformatory for youthful offenders.

There is no experience to match that of having

your freedom taken away from you and your life not being yours to control any longer. I felt things could not get any worse, but they did. One day I was called to the prison chaplain's office. He sat me down and looked in my face and told me my mother had called on the phone to ask him to tell me that my brother Butch had died of a drug overdose.

That night I cried for my brother like I'd never cried before. A few days later I was allowed to go to his wake. But I had to be escorted by a prison guard, and I had to wear handcuffs. It was very hard to look at my brother as he lay in his coffin, knowing I would never see him smile or laugh again.

Being sent to prison and the death of my brother ended my childhood. . . .

Ben Bates

Ben Bates is the head of the English department of Langston University in Langston, Oklahoma, where he lives with his wife and two children. He is the author of several published short stories and a play.

Having grown up in a racially segregated environment in Chicago, Ben says that he was conditioned early on to see things from a racial perspective. "I think I paid too much attention to race when I was younger," he says. "When I went to college I wanted to be a lawyer because I felt obliged to serve 'my people.' I think black people are too diverse and have too many interests for such a simpleminded notion. I would have been better off pursuing more personal concerns. Anything black people do is a black thing."

In this personally revealing story, Ben describes the particular challenges of his coming of age as "an affirmative-action baby."

BOOMERISM, OR
DOING TIME IN THE IVY LEAGUE

My friend Jackie made partner in a big Chicago law firm a couple of years ago. She started with nothing; now she needs tax shelters. She thinks the story of "those hoodlum children who went to the Ivy League in the sixties and seventies" has not been told. I think Jackie is right, but I am not the one to tell the story. I haven't maintained much contact with my Yale classmates. I think of Yale as I think of my first marriage. (Yes, I actually married a Yale woman.) From courtship to marriage to dissolution, we spent about five years as a Yale couple. Yet, at this writing, we haven't spoken in at least ten years. I wouldn't know where to find her—or why I might want to. Back then I thought she would be the most important person in my life.

The hoodlum children are also known as affirmative-action babies. When the elite institutions opened their doors to us thirty years ago, it was a symbol of liberation. Today, having a handful of black lawyers and doctors doesn't seem quite so revolutionary. The hoodlum children have come a long way. But it has been a strange trip—more hallucination than dream.

In high school I wasn't even a hoodlum. During the winter and spring of 1968 I was the first-ever junior class president at Harlan High School in Chicago, immersed in plans for our first-ever junior prom. Before 1968, only seniors received such privileges as proms and presidents, but our class was different. Change was in the air. We were breaking new ground. I was a young black boy at an almost all-black high school, thinking, "Today the junior class, tomorrow the nation!" I wore an iridescent blue Nehru jacket to that first prom.

I was in tune with the times. Nineteen sixty-eight was perhaps the only time in American history when a young black boy who expressed such an ambition was as likely to be encouraged as ridiculed. Martin Luther King Jr. had expressed dreams far more grand five years earlier. Lyndon Johnson had said, "We shall overcome." Congress and the courts had attacked the separate-but-equal doctrine. Hundreds of thousands of my elders had negotiated, marched, sung, shouted, demanded, and died. Why couldn't I be president? If I played my cards right, a talented young fellow like me could even—go to Yale!

And so it came to pass. A man named G. H. Walker, stockbroker and Yale alumnus, employed a black lawyer named Benjamin Duster as his scout. Duster knew Silas Purnell, who ran a college counseling agency out of his basement in the

Dearborn Homes housing project. Purnell knew the guidance counselor at Harlan High School, Ms. Richey, who knew me: junior class president, owner of a set of killer (for a young black boy) SAT scores, son of a factory worker and a postal clerk. Me, who didn't know what a stock was or why people bought them.

G. H. Walker took the Branch Rickey approach. In 1947, the Brooklyn Dodgers already had a (segregated) system for player development. Rickey could have scoured his own minor leagues for years and never found a Jackie Robinson. Instead, he removed his blinders and stepped into a new talent pool. Soon, other owners signed Negro Leaguers because they wanted to compete, not to do favors for black men. Rickey took affirmative action to improve his team; G. H. Walker did the same. I was one of eight young black boys who met with Duster in Purnell's basement office. They encouraged us to apply to Yale and told us that Walker's sponsorship could make the difference between admission and rejection.

I don't recall ever meeting Mr. Walker. Perhaps we shook hands once. When I think of him today, a blend of the Wizard of Oz and Mr. Norton from Ralph Ellison's *Invisible Man* comes to mind: pale, frail, with thinning white hair and watery blue eyes behind rimless glasses, charcoal-gray suit, white shirt, striped tie, working the strings on my shoulders. But this is not a real memory. As a high school senior, I had not read Ralph Ellison. And I'd never been to Oz until a fine September evening in 1969, when I walked through the Vanderbilt Gate onto the Old Campus of Yale for the first time and saw on my right a group of about twenty students, kicking up dust in competition for a huge blooper ball; on my left, fluid groupings of two and five and eight and ten, talking, laughing, hugging, whistling, waving; and the air full of boomerangs, Frisbees, and balls. Oh, my.

I knew I wasn't in Kansas anymore, but then I'd never been to Kansas, either. I'd never been much of anywhere beyond Chicago's south side. My father, from Alabama, and my mother, from Arkansas, came to Chicago with millions of other migrants before World War II. They learned, as did most southern blacks who came north, that their lives in the north were no less separate and no more equal than they were in the south.

My parents met, married, and raised three sons during an era when Chicago was known as the most segregated city in America. We were not isolated on the South Side, any more than the slaves were truly isolated from the slave owners, but our excursions—to Wrigley Field or Comiskey Park, to the museums, to the Loop—always had the feel of maneuvers behind enemy lines. We learned to shrug at the snarled insult of some bus driver, to feel guilty when some matron's knees buckled as we brushed (barely!) past her on our way to the toy department at Marshall Field's. On family outings and school field trips—especially those that would bring us in contact with whites—we were scrubbed, groomed, and pressed to the hilt, and ordered to be on our best behavior. Kindnesses from whites were not uncommon, but we always anticipated bigotry. Nevertheless, we were happy.

Our happiness could be measured in part by the relief we felt after a foray into the city, when we returned to the comfort and security of segregation.

But in the late sixties, change was in the air. Today, we remember the events as catalysts. We say that the assassinations, or the riots, changed our way of thinking. But maybe change spreads like a virus. And events are signs of infection. First the virus infiltrates the emotions. A strange mood takes hold of the victim. He feels *different*. Destined for greatness. All things seem possible. A poor black boy can become president. Then the victim is overwhelmed by a mix of ambition and despair. He feels inspired, when in fact he is quite ill. Deviant behavior follows.

If this seems too speculative, consider a comment Lyndon Johnson made when *Time* named him Man of the Year for 1967:

> *In all candor, I cannot recall a period that is in any way comparable to the one we are living through today. It is a period that finds exhilaration and frustration going hand in hand—when great accomplishments are often overshadowed by rapidly rising expectations.*
>
> ("LBJ as Lear," *Time*, 5 January, 1968: 13-22)

Johnson describes the early stages of the "boomerism" syndrome. The illness is characterized by paradox. For my parents' generation, their children's bright prospects were a source of joy and, when they thought of their own separate-but-equal experience, bitterness. Sometimes the contradictions were too much to bear. This may explain why calls for fair treatment, for equal opportunity, could sound like threats. This March, 1968, report of events in Memphis is boomerism full-blown:

Last week Memphis simmered on the rim of racial rampage . . . What began a month ago as a walkout by city employees is now a black and white confrontation. Memphis garbage collectors, most of them making $1.80 an hour, went on strike . . . Nearly all of Memphis's 1300 garbage men are black . . . Mayor Henry Loeb has spurned the strikers' demands . . . Invoking Tennessee court decisions banning strikes by public service workers, the mayor brought in some 150 strikebreakers. The Negro community countered with a boycott of downtown stores with the slogan: "No new clothes for Easter." Seven hundred Negroes picnicked in City Hall. A few youngsters tried to overturn a police cruiser. Nervous cops sprayed the kids' faces with Mace. Injunctions were brought against union leaders. When a contingent of Negro ministers and militants returned to City Hall, a raucous exchange of words resulted in the arrest of 117 protesters . . . 200 youngsters invaded the steps of City Hall to hold a mock *funeral, solemnly burying justice in a borrowed gray casket. Young raiders broke into a Beale Street department store. Fires were set to the garbage piling up at a rate of nearly 500 tons a day . . . "I am not in favor of violence," said the Rev. James M. Lawson, Jr., an erudite militant who leads much of the Negro struggle. But "if I were inclined to advocate burning, it would be in East Memphis [where the mayor lives]—I think we've had enough talk of this burning down our own neighborhoods."*

("Memphis," *Time*, 15 March 1968: 19-26)

In this setting, Martin Luther King Jr.'s assassination during the first week of April in 1968, seems more climax than catalyst.

After King's murder, I found the nerve to tell my parents that I wanted to wear an Afro. We spent most of my senior year of high school debating haircuts. My parents also objected to my involvement in the Black Student Federation, a short-lived spin-off of Operation Breadbasket, which later became Operation PUSH. I traveled the South Side and the West Side making speeches to whomever showed up. Our mission was to organize the high school students in the struggle against racism. I even made a speech, that spring of 1969, to the Operation Breadbasket Saturday morning meeting and had an across-the-lunch-table conversation with the Reverend Jesse Jackson. I don't remember a word that was said, but at the time I felt as if I had been anointed. I would really let my hair grow when I got to Yale.

My uncle Dudley came to visit me that first semester in New Haven. In my family, Uncle Dudley was the prosperous one. He drove a Cadillac and always wore a coat and tie. He was the first person I knew who had a flash timer and could get into his own photographs. As I was growing up, he had never consistently gotten my name right, but that day I was the apple of his eye. He made good use of the flash timer, setting up his shots and then throwing an arm around me in front of my Farnam Hall entryway, in the Pierson College dining hall, in Beinecke Plaza. . . . In every shot my bushy head sits atop a sweatshirt that looks three sizes too small. It was my only clean article of clothing that said "Yale," and my uncle Dudley insisted I wear it. At home, he was a dignified, autocratic figure, but that day he was thrilled just to walk the campus with me. He looked as if he had been in the Negro Leagues for years and finally, vicariously, he was playing in the majors. I didn't know what his business was, but I thought he would have given up everything he owned for the chance to be a Yalie.

In retrospect, Uncle Dudley's infection seems obvious, but at the time I didn't see it. I couldn't understand how he could be a somebody *and* a nobody. This disorientation (Uncle Dudley's and mine) is another symptom of the virus.

Many of the young black men and women who arrived on campus that fall shared Uncle Dudley's enthusiasm. They cultivated white friendships, let the brothers and sisters slide. They told themselves: "Now you can be a doctor, a lawyer, a doctorlawyer! This is your chance. Make your connections. Now you too can have a Yale degree. Now you can join the corporations. Now you can have a suburban, no, a country home. Now you can live. Like white people." Some of the blacks I met at Yale had escaped the Negro Leagues long ago, knew better than to look back, yet were still vulnerable to infection. Once, I spent most of my time at a freshman mixer stalking a woman who, according to campus lore, had never been seen speaking to another black person. "She must think she white!" was how some folks put it. You couldn't call what we had a conversation, but I breathed all over her.

Some of us knew we could never be white and feared that we would never measure up, that we didn't really belong in the major leagues. In the summer of 1997, we celebrated the Negro Leagues, but nobody, then or now, thinks of the Negro Leagues as first class. Josh Gibson may have hit 972 home runs, but he is not the home run king. The affirmative-action conflict revolves around a shared assumption about the difference between first class and second class. On one side is the idea that privileges (such as the chance to "play in the majors") should be shared, or at least distributed fairly; on the other side is the idea that privileges must be preserved and protected. Both sides are concerned that first-class institutions not be "watered down" by people who "don't belong." A comment in *Newsweek* from Supreme Court justice Clarence Thomas on his experience at Yale Law School expresses the tension created by this debate:

> *You had to prove yourself every day because the presumption was that you were dumb and didn't deserve to be there on merit.*
> ("Supreme Mystery," *Newsweek*, 9 September 1991: 27-34.)

When the virus strikes, the ambition to "prove yourself" feels exactly like the fear that your inferiority will be exposed. Thomas is a walking illustration of the fine line between inspiration and illness. Some affirmative-action babies found the "compensatory" programs, the "remediations" that enabled them to partake of privilege, quite salutary. Other carriers of the virus found these same "support services" debilitating. Then there were those, such as the justice, who suffered a dual effect, and found themselves simultaneously uplifted and insulted. Paradox is the signature of boomerism.

Some of us at Yale knew that we could never be white and celebrated. In a swift series of roommate swaps and evictions, one group of brothers resegregated an entryway in Wright Hall that fall of 1969. This area became known as the Ghetto. The brothers from the Ghetto ate together, partied together, chased women together, played cards together, studied together (occasionally!), and kept each other's backs against the white menace.

They told themselves: "These people don't want us here, except maybe as entertainment. They think we can all sing, dance, or bounce a ball. We ain't going for it. The white man lies. Been lying about black people, lying to black people, since day one. We ain't going for it." In the Ghetto, they refused to believe that the Ivy League—Uncle Dudley's Ivy League—was real; more likely, it was some kind of trick. The Ghetto brothers were more than college students—they were revolutionaries. One of the Ghetto's leading residents meticulously redesigned the "Yale" on his notebooks and folders to read "Jail."

Blame it on the virus. The college student who sees himself as political prisoner is a classic victim of boomerism. In him we see how the syndrome clouds the judgment, causes delusions of grandeur. I speak as a survivor of the plague.

My personal crisis began when I visited the Yale Co-Op for the first time. I was out of my element. The best measure of the distance between the South Side and the Ivy League is that I had budgeted one hundred dollars for my books and figured I'd have spending money left over. When I spent seventy-five dollars that first time through the line, on books for one course, I felt like a fish flapping around on the dock. In rapid order, it occurred to me that my parents couldn't help me, that I was in class with the sons and daughters of rich white folks, that I could never make it without my books (my books!), that my glorious future was in jeopardy, that maybe, somehow, I had been tricked. Very shortly thereafter I learned that the brothers from the Ghetto also stole books together.

As I write this, the Yale Co-Op, like every other college bookstore, is a marvel of electronic surveillance, but in the days of the hoodlum children this was not so. Back then, the Co-Op was a garden, the fruit was ripe, you could pick it yourself. The managers of the Co-Op believed in an honor code; the brothers from the Ghetto thought the whole thing was stupid. You could enter the Co-Op empty-handed, pick out a high-priced leather briefcase, fill it with books, and walk. I was never that flamboyant. I preferred to take two or three books at a time and leave the store openly with the books in my hand. I could do just as well as the briefcase boys by making multiple trips.

This was revolutionary shoplifting. I reasoned that if I was expected to compete with rich Yalies, my access to the textbooks should be as easy as theirs. I was merely compensating for my disadvantage. I only stole books (and high-quality plastic playing cards, which were the rage), but I didn't limit myself to assigned readings. I stole books with titles that intrigued me. I stole books for my less revolutionary friends. I stole books to impress women. I stole the books that I thought an educated young man should have, two or three at a time, no fidgeting, no skulking looks behind me as I exited the store.

They didn't stop me until my sophomore year, when I was on the way out of the store with two books: *The Triumph of Conservatism*, by Gabriel Kolko, which I needed for a U.S. history course, and *Passing*, a Harlem Renaissance novel by Nella Larsen. Just outside the Co-Op door, a security guard said, "Wait a minute. Did you pay for those books?"

"Yeah."

"I don't think so."

"What are you talking about?"

"You're going to have to come with me."

I was taken to a back room and left to sweat. A few minutes later, the security guard came in with a manager. I stuck to my story. After I went back and forth with the guard a few times, the manager spoke. "You were seen taking these books from the shelf."

"I don't know what you saw, but I came into this store with these books."

"You just walked into the store with two new books, then turned around and walked out?"

"That's right."

"So why did you come into the store?" The manager thought he had me. One corner of his mouth turned up.

"I need a couple of other books, but I can't afford them."

Now the manager looked as if his fish had gotten off the hook. He motioned to the security guard, and they left the room. Then the security guard returned. "You can leave now."

"Can I take my books?"

"Take them and get the hell out of here!" The

security guard looked at me, but I don't think he saw me. I took the books and left, calmly. Somehow I had turned a lie into the truth. Or maybe it was the other way around.

I told my story in the Ghetto and received congratulations from the brothers. I tried to convince myself that I had won a battle. I continued to steal books from the Co-Op, refining my technique, becoming an expert literary shoplifter. When I was stopped again in my junior year, and spent a few hours in a jail cell, it was just the price of doing business. Somebody from the college bailed me out. I was on my way to great things. As a senior, I met my first wife.

Today, whenever I walk through a sensing device in a library or bookstore, a department store at the mall; whenever I walk through a metal detector at the airport or in a public high school, I consider it a tangible legacy of the hoodlum children. It appears that the affirmative-action debate has already been decided. We want protection from the virus. This is no time for stories about the ambitions of poor black youth.

LeVan D. Hawkins

———◆———

LeVan D. Hawkins, who lives in West Hollywood, California, has written for the *Los Angeles Weekly*, the *Los Angeles Times*, the *Sacramento News and Review*, and the *Santa Fe Reporter*.

In this story about his freshman year of college, he exposes the racial humiliation that he endured at the hands of his white roommate, Fred [a pseudonym]. Still, even though his focus is on white racism, LeVan carefully points out that he had felt the same kind of humiliation in the past, when black high school classmates frequently told him he was "too white." "Black people had given me a tremendous amount of grief, too," he says, "and I'd become accustomed to abuse."

LeVan is very clear that he doesn't want to be pitied for being black, and he doesn't want to live his life in reaction to racial oppression. "If I constantly find myself reacting to it, I will never be free," he says. "I still stand up to any injustice I experience; I just stand up from a position of strength."

LeVan believes that he has an obligation to serve as "a bridge between races, sexes, sexualities, and religions," and that it is especially important to reach out to young people.

FRED

When I was a freshman in college, I could only listen to the music I loved when my roommate, Fred, left the room. This was in the mid-seventies. We used record players—stereos—then. I didn't have one; Fred did and he hated black music.

"Don't want to hear it. Don't have to—it's my record player."

I couldn't understand why he was so opposed to hearing my music. My taste in music wasn't radical, nor did the singers sing lyrics denigrating whites. I liked black pop—The Stylistics, Barry White, Aretha Franklin, Marvin Gaye—great music made by black artists that appealed to people of all colors. Fred, however, was the exception, and he had the power—he owned the stereo. If I wanted to play the few albums I owned or to listen to the rhythm-and-blues radio station that played the music I enjoyed, I had to wait until he was out of the room to do it.

I suppose some people wouldn't have used his stereo under those conditions, but I loved music—I had to hear it. Every morning, I woke with a song playing in my head, and I listened passionately to the radio and kept top-ten lists of my favorite current records.

Fred loved music, too. On numerous occasions, he excitedly played his favorite music for me. His choice of music was white rock and pop.

"This is good stuff."

Some of it was. I enjoyed it and I told him so. When I tried to share my music with him, he derided it.

"All that hoo-hooing and stuff!" He would make sounds and dance around the room. "Hoo-hoo! Hoo-hoo!"

Once he grabbed one of my Aretha Franklin albums and spotted white pop star Elton John's name listed as one of the songwriters. "These people can't even write their own music."

Aretha is one of the most acclaimed singers in the history of contemporary music, but to Fred she was inferior. For him, a black singer or group's singing songs written by white rock and pop stars was proof of the superiority of white music. My way of responding was to say, "I like what I like. You like what you like." I wish I had known what I learned as an adult: The singers and groups he was telling me to listen to, the "classics"—the Rolling Stones, Eric Clapton, and the Beatles—all based their sounds on African-American musicians who had gone before them.

When I was completing my application for college housing, I came across the question, "Do you have any preference in roommates?" I wrote "no." It never occurred to me to write "black," as I later discovered many blacks had. I had attended an integrated high school of blacks and whites in my junior and senior years and had many white friends, so the idea of a white roommate didn't alarm me; I would take whatever roommate I was assigned—it would be an adventure!

It was. A bad one.

If Fred wasn't ridiculing my music, he was ridiculing the way I spoke.

"I thought you were going to the library," he said to me one day when he entered the room.

"I have to go downtown. I figured I'd go then."

He moved toward me.

"You'll go when?" he asked, smiling.

"Huh?" I had no idea what was so humorous.

"You'll go 'then.' " He mocked me. Eyes gleaming, a big smile spread across his face, he bobbed his head as he stood in my face and exaggeratedly pronounced "then" as if it was the exact rhyme of "tin."

"'Then,'" he laughed, his body rocking in spasms.

One night, around the same period, I sat at a dinner party, the lone black, and told a story about my grandmother. A woman interrupted me and corrected my grammar.

"My God, speak the King's English," she said indignantly. Angry and embarrassed, I became quiet. The room was silent; all eyes were on me. I awkwardly continued and hurried the story to its conclusion. I didn't know what king the woman was referring to, but I knew that she and Fred had the same one. Their message was clear: The way I spoke was wrong.

That was the same message I received when I started high school, except the bullies who beat and harassed me (all black) accused me of trying to "sound white." At that time, I had never been around any white people—I lived in an all-black town and went to all-black schools until I was in the eleventh grade.

Fred's constant ridicule wore me down. I began to speak at a slow, deliberate pace to make sure I didn't make any mistakes. Speaking became a chore.

"Boy! What's wrong with you!" he'd ask, accenting the "boy."

Boy was the nickname he assigned me, always said with a laugh and a smile. I knew he knew enough American history to know that years ago black men had been mistreated and had been called Boy by white men half their age. Never Mister, never by their names. Boy. It was demeaning. The word "boy" spoken by a white man to a black man carries memories of degradation and oppression. Those days were supposed to be over. And here was this white man doing it to me, except he did it with a smile, and when I told him to stop, he'd tell me it was a nickname and that I should "feel like part of the group."

I wrote a term paper for my English class entitled "The Immigrant." In it, I wrote that since I started college, I felt like an immigrant in my own country—a man without a land; displaced behind language and cultural barriers. I handed Fred the paper, hoping he'd understand how I felt and change his behavior. Instead he flew into a rage.

"It's a pack of lies! I don't treat you like that! I treat you like one of the guys. Guys razz each other."

I didn't mind being teased. I resented that the names and jokes were always related to color. I had been stripped of my identity.

In high school, I was recognized as an honor student; an actor. The bullies called me a sissy. All these identities were based upon my personality and behavior. When I was Fred's roommate, I was reduced to just a color, something I possessed from birth.

Out of the thirty thousand students who attended my college, only three thousand were black. Whenever I saw another black student, I would nod or say "Hey" or "What's happening?" It helped us feel less lonely. Blacks also ate at the "black table" in the cafeteria, a table where all the blacks sat and had conversations without being ridiculed about the way they spoke. That is, as long as they sounded "black."

I don't know why I didn't sit there.

I think some of it had to do with spending the first two years of high school fighting off bullies who were black like me. When I moved to an integrated school, where whites made up seventy-five percent of the enrollment, I was relieved; most of the bullies dropped out, and the remaining ones started terrorizing the white students, who wouldn't fight back, so I was left alone. Still the beatings, the harassment, had left their impact. I knew that every black person was not my friend. Race was not the only requirement for friendship.

The idea of separatism bothered me. The black table was such a visible antisocial statement. Still, if the others had relationships with their roommates like the one I had with Fred, I understood.

If I could have stopped Fred from the actions I thought were offensive, we would've had a great relationship. We had long discussions about life, told jokes to each other, and had common goals. I knew it was possible for us to get beyond race. Doug, one of my best friends in high school, was white. Occasionally, we would discuss race or he would tell me some stupid racial joke he heard, but we never ridiculed each other because of our cultural differences.

I usually went to dinner with Fred and the people who lived in the rooms near us. The idea of sitting at a table full of strangers horrified me, so I stayed where it was familiar.

Some of the blacks didn't like it and wrote graffiti on the study-hall wall calling me an Uncle Tom and a traitor to my race. It hurt. I was ashamed and I questioned whether it was true. When I went home for the holidays, I constantly talked to my brother about it.

"I wouldn't worry about it," he told me. He also attended an integrated high school. "Just be true to yourself. You can't care what people think." It was good advice. Unfortunately, I cared.

I should have expected the ostracizing. I knew the rules. At the integrated high school I attended, there were unwritten rules regarding associating with white people. One of them was that a black person should never sit alone with a white person or a group of whites at a public gathering; you had to have another black person with you. In high school, I never disobeyed that rule. In college, I was always the lone black at our dinner table.

One day, Fred came home and told me that he had seen the graffiti in the study hall. He found it amusing. I looked at him in hatred and amazement.

You're the reason they call me that, I thought. And you're not worth it.

When winter break neared, I called home and asked my ex-boss if I could work at my old job during my vacation. It was a harsh Midwestern winter; sub-zero temperatures and heavy snows. I worked the midnight shift and drove to work when the mercury dropped to its lowest. One night, my car slid on the ice that blanketed the street and I ended up stuck helplessly in a ditch.

I would rather have been in my warm home resting in my comfortable bed, but I was determined to make some money: I was going to buy a stereo. I drove to work fantasizing about turning it up to its highest volume and blasting Fred out of the room. Aretha Franklin blasting out the Rolling Stones. It was what motivated me during those cold midnight rides.

The stereo I bought was flashy, with blue, yellow, and red fluorescent lights that moved with the music. It was loaded down with knobs and gadgets I had no idea how to use, and it was huge—one of the reasons I bought it. It dwarfed Fred's tiny, plain black stereo when I placed it on his desk.

I sat on my bed, put my hands behind my head, and waited for him. He entered the room, said hello, and put his coat and suitcase in the closet. I smiled and waited patiently. When he turned, he saw it. He looked at me. I smirked. He smiled in pain and walked toward my stereo.

"Wow." He looked at me again.

The smirk was still on my face.

"I'm sure you'll be fair," he said. He unplugged his stereo and placed it in the closet.

He was right. I was fair. I listened to my music whenever I wanted and allowed him to listen to his. I no longer had to wait until he left the room. No longer had to ask for his permission. The power had shifted.

When I think about that day, I ask myself why he assumed I would be fair. It would have been a very human reaction to treat him as he had treated me. But I let it go because I knew how it felt. It was degrading. It hurt: waiting until he left the room to listen to the radio; being called Boy; watching him while he ridiculed my writing ability; listening to him mock the way I spoke. I knew how unfairness felt, so I was fair.

I learned valuable lessons from Fred. I learned to listen to music with my heart and ears open. I learned to respect people's differences and that differences don't mean a person is inferior—or superior, for that matter. I learned that if you have to depend upon another person to supply you with what you need, it gives that person too much power. I also learned that people in power usually wait until they're losing it before they start talking about fairness.

Crystal Ann Williams

A widely published writer who lives in Ithaca, New York, Crystal Ann Williams says her work is about "personal revolution through revelation." In this short short story she spotlights a painful, racially motivated event in her childhood. "What happened to me that day was horrible and shameful," she says. "And, more important, it still happens—every day to colored people in every city, every state in these United States of America."

IN THE BELLY OF A CLOTHES RACK

The air is sweet with a new clothes smell, still, and so dry your nostrils contract.

Whenever we shopped, Momma and me, I would hide in the bellies of clothes racks. I liked sitting there looking up at the dropped ceiling as the dimmed fluorescent light filtered down through clothes that people had tossed. And I counted. I counted how many tags pushed their way toward me, how many one-armed hangers fell on me, and how many manicured nails twisted hangers off the rack.

I liked listening, too. There were heels clicking, muted voices whispering, and Momma's voice, humming softly, drifting over the racks to my cocooned ears. I pretended to be a crouched tigress, unseen and unheard, but hearing and hunting, placing myself at the throats of shoppers, trying to anticipate their next move. That day, a daughter pleaded, her voice gathered at the edge of hysteria, "But, Mother . . . I just can't wear that." It was a good game, to wonder from whose lips the words had come.

Saks Fifth Avenue was my favorite because it was library-quiet. There were no children shrieking or threatening to encroach on my world of beige sleeves and price tags. There was no being bumped by elbows, no trailing behind my mother as she shopped. It was a good deal—Momma knew where I was and I knew where she was, her humming a buoy.

I should have been listening for Momma, but I was too busy pouting about the cold ice and the blood I could still taste on the inside of my lip after my failed attempt at a double lutz. So when I readjusted my ears and realized that there was no humming, I scrambled out of the clothes rack and stood on tiptoe trying to find her. But I was too short.

So I jumped up and down, my feet pounding the vanilla tile. That didn't work either, so I stood and called until all sound shrank, in a receding crouch, from my body. She wasn't there. I couldn't see. There was nothing but my shrill voice begging for Momma.

Frozen in the middle of the ladies' dresses department, I remembered Momma's words: "If we ever get separated, just stay put. I'll find you." So that's what I did. My eyes searched the aisles, finding only a little girl in a pink-and-blue sundress who collided with her mother, who had stopped short to glare at me. A security guard who looked like my cousin Mack, his dark face surrounding Barbie-doll-red lips, stood at his post near the down escalator, a short distance away, beckoning. And then my pupils darkened and were filled with a stern-faced, spectacled white woman.

"Little girl, what is it you're doing?" she hissed.

"Looking for my mother."

"Your mother is not here."

"Yes she is. She's here. She was just here."

"Girl!" Her head tilted down, allowing her eyes to peer over the racks and then back to me. "There is no one here who could be your mother. She certainly isn't here." And then under her breath she whispered, "And what would she be doing if she were?"

Her face was angular. Her hair was brown and short and haphazardly placed. Her suit was blue. A delicate Jesus swayed across her chest. The lapel pin she wore glinted in the faded light.

It was then, when I was seven, on that Saturday afternoon at the Saks in Fairland Mall, in Dearborn, Michigan, that I knew that the clarity of my family—my father's black, leathery skin, the smooth milk of my mother's white skin, and the brown sugar of my skin—was obscured. The saleswoman didn't understand, but I did. I knew the implication. I'd seen it before, but I hadn't known what it was, hadn't known it was directed at me.

Even as I could hear Momma's "Cris? Crissy?!" I understood what being lost meant. Being lost is to look in the face of a spectacled white woman and wonder what the gnarled ball making its way from your stomach to your throat is called.

Charisse Nesbit

———◆———

It seemed that I was too black for the white people, yet not black enough for the black people,"
Charisse Nesbit says in her account of growing up
in Maryland in the 1970s and 1980s. Echoing a
familiar theme, Charisse depicts her search for a
community in which she could be herself—free to
dress, act, and talk as she saw fit. After a stint at
the University of New Mexico, where she continued to suffer at the hands of those who called her
"white girl," she finally found solace in Atlanta's
black community.

CHILD OF THE DREAM

I was always called "white girl" as a child—and maybe I was. After all, I was a product of my environment. I was brought up with white Barbie dolls of impossible proportions and long silky blond hair—neither of which I possessed. As a child, I believed what I was taught, and I wasn't taught to love myself for who I am—an African-American.

Growing up in a mixed neighborhood in rural Maryland, I had to deal with white people all the time. Although we all interacted on a daily basis, the white children in my classes knew nothing about me as a black person. This revelation occurred to me one day when I was in the sixth grade. I was talking with three classmates, two white girls and one black boy. We were talking about washing our hair, when the boy mentioned that I didn't wash my hair every day. I began to explain why, but the girls cut me off.

"You don't wash your hair every day? I would feel so dirty if I didn't wash my hair every day. Ewww!"

I went on to explain that my hair was different and that I couldn't wash it every day, but it didn't matter. Being a kid, I didn't have the knowledge to explain the difference in our hair types and the fact that my hair didn't make enough natural oil to be washed every day. (Later I understood all this from having to deal with my hair and its complications.) All my classmates understood, in that five minutes of conversation, was that I was a black girl with bad hygiene.

This made me question myself. Was I dirty? I knew I wasn't, but because I couldn't explain myself well enough, I began to feel as though I was and that those girls had unearthed something about me that I had just never realized. It wasn't until much later in life that I realized that their thinking was wrong but, in the meantime, I tried to convince myself that a whole race of people, most of whom only washed their hair once a week, could not be wrong.

In middle school I discovered magazines that featured black women. It was important for me to have these images of glamorous black women, which I'd craved so long, and I would sometimes carry the magazines to school. One day in eighth grade I had one of the magazines open to a relaxer ad featuring a woman with very smooth, beautiful hair—in my opinion, anyway. A white classmate looked over my shoulder and pointed out the picture to another classmate. "Do you think she uses thirty-weight or forty-weight on her hair?" Thinking this very funny, he howled with laughter.

Previously, when this boy had touched my hair and found it somewhat slick, I'd tried to explain to him why I used hair grease. This time, I simply told him that African-Americans didn't use car oil on their hair and that our hair wasn't naturally oily like white people's hair. I was tired of blatant ignorance and having to constantly justify who I was and why I did the things I did.

Nevertheless, I used to pray every night that I would somehow miraculously wake up with long, silky, wash-and-go hair like my Barbie's. I would even go so far as to put a towel on my head, pretending I had hair that would swing like the white girls' hair at school—far different from my Afro puffs, which wouldn't budge when the strongest winds would blow.

Just washing and combing our hair, when it is in its natural state, is a chore that can take hours. As a child, getting my hair done became a bonding process between my mother and me, mainly because it took so long to do. We'd spend the time together talking and swapping stories, learning a lot about each other. My classmates could never have known how much it hurt me to have them criticize my grooming habits and ridicule something that meant so much to me. And because I wasn't able to explain, I just held it inside and tried to work it out within myself.

I constantly questioned myself as a child. All of the positive images of people I'd seen were white. To be beautiful, you not only had to be stick-skinny, with no behind, you had to have long silky blond hair and blue eyes, a thin nose, and thin lips. I'd look in the mirror at my full lips, flat nose, brown eyes, and kinky black hair and feel like I just didn't measure up. I didn't look a thing like Barbie, not even when they came out with the black versions, which still had blue eyes and were basically just a darker version of the white one. Because I didn't fit the mold, I had a hard time convincing myself that I was beautiful.

To get away from these stark realities, I'd often turn to books. The fantasies portrayed in them offered me the opportunity to lose myself for a little while, but all the books I read growing up were about white people. I used to enjoy the Sweet Valley High series about two Barbie-like twins, Elizabeth and Jessica, who drove a fancy car and had perfect suburban lives. This series, and others like it, influenced me so much that, when I first began writing, all of my stories featured white characters. I didn't feel it was possible to have characters who were black because everything I'd read featured only white characters.

I had teachers who tried to get me to read stories by black authors, but since the teachers were white, I saw them as trying to pigeonhole me into only reading about black characters. So, if anything, instead of opening me up to a whole world of authors I could relate to, their efforts only served to push me away from black authors. I never saw them pushing black authors on the white kids, so when they pushed them on me, I saw them as trying to make me fit into yet another stereotype.

Most of the programs I watched on television were also about white people. In fact, the only time I'd see African-Americans was when one of us portrayed a hooker or a criminal. Often, the black-criminal drama would be acted out in real life on the news when I'd see a black man getting hauled away in handcuffs.

Wanting something more for myself than what seemed to be my fate, I began to identify with the way of life I'd read about in Sweet Valley High. I didn't deny I was an African-American, but I decided I didn't have to talk in slang, be uneducated, or act uncivilized or unruly to keep my identity.

Everyone else where I lived felt otherwise, however. Taking their cues from stereotypes they saw on television, they began to call me "white girl" or "wannabe" because I refused to be a stereotypical African-American. These names hurt, as did the ignorance I'd gotten from the white kids, only more. I could understand the white kids' ignorance regarding who I was. They had never been forced to learn about my culture the way I was forced to learn about theirs. What I couldn't understand was how my own people could purposely say things to hurt me. We had all been through the same thing. Why did they hate me for being a little different? Sounding educated and being interested in things other than what they were interested in didn't make me any less black, did it? It seemed that I was too black for white people, yet not black enough for black people.

I thought that if I was going to be free to be myself, without having to feel bad for it, I was going to have to go away to school and experience a different culture. I thought I'd be able to do that in New Mexico. But going to a different place, especially one with a very low number of African-Americans, only served to make me start the process of proving myself all over again. Because I wore my hair differently from the other African-Americans on campus and dressed a little differently and didn't speak slang, I came under scrutiny by my people once again.

It wasn't enough for them that I was obviously black and made no effort to hide or deny my blackness. They still pointed the finger and accused me of being white-washed. Even though most of them had been raised by white people and knew less about our shared heritage than I did, they still decided to make up their minds about who I was before they actually got to know me. Once again, I was not "black enough."

When I confronted a guy at a black student union meeting about this, he said, "You're just trying to be white. You talk white, you look white, you smell white." Everyone in the room was shocked, and most of them tried to stifle their surprised laughter, but it didn't matter. The damage was done. Once again I was the victim of ignorance and misunderstanding. I "smelled white"?

I began to hear echoes of voices from my past—accusations of trying to be something I wasn't—only they weren't from my past. It was bad memories repeating themselves all over again.

Finally, after going on an academic exchange for a year to Atlanta and taking a break from the University of New Mexico, I experienced things that transformed me, and I finally saw images I thought only existed in my wildest dreams. It was there that I realized that, although people I'd met had treated me as though I were a stranger to my own race because of my differences, I really wasn't.

Atlanta taught me that there were African-Americans who knew of a world beyond what was shown to them on television. There I met and made friends with entrepreneurs, medical students, and aspiring musicians—all black. My friends and I would stroll through the most expensive malls in Atlanta, stopping to play the pianos in the stores without thinking twice, even though most of the patrons in the malls were white. This was something that would never have happened anywhere else I'd lived. I had always been self-conscious about being black—especially when shopping anywhere expensive.

In Atlanta I realized that it is okay to know who you are and what you want and to actively and aggressively pursue your dream, regardless of what it is. I realized that even the most farfetched dream is available to me, not just reserved for white people. Meeting the people I met in Atlanta made me realize that I wasn't alone in wanting more out of life than what was offered to those of my race on television. They made me realize, finally, that wanting and getting things by using my intellect did not make me any less black or any more white.

Despite what is shown on television and in magazines, successful, educated black people (some of whom have no sense of rhythm) do exist. Their success doesn't make them any less black or mean that they have forgotten who they are as black people. Seeing them, I no longer feel bad about trying to do something with myself and leaving my friends behind in Maryland to do nothing with themselves.

I'm proud of who I am as a person and what I'm doing with my life. Because I am graduated from college and speak the way I do, I still hear the occasional talk of "white girl"—but it is only occasional now. I have to do what's best for me by being me and not what someone else feels I should be. I've learned to love myself for who I am, a black woman who is beautiful in her own right and who looks nothing at all like Barbie.

Mia Threlkeld

With an honesty that might astonish many adults, fourteen-year-old Mia Threlkeld of Birmingham, Alabama, writes of her experience of having other black teenagers label her too white. While she has moved beyond caring about her peers' racial remarks—chalking them up to ignorance—she thinks that black and white people have a long way to go in regard to racism.

Still, Mia says, she doesn't want any special privileges. "I actually think affirmative action adds to the racism problem today," she says. "I don't want white people to start thinking that blacks can't get anywhere in this world without special treatment."

All the names in her story, except her own, have been changed.

A TRUE FRIEND?

My name is Mia, and I am a fourteen-year-old black female from Birmingham, Alabama. I like all people no matter what their skin color. I'm against racism, and it really upsets me when I see racists because it is like they are missing out on meeting a lot of great people just because they are afraid of anything that is different from themselves. You can't blame the people themselves, though, because you are not born racist—you are raised that way by your parents or you are influenced by your friends. I think if we all could see everyone through our hearts instead of our eyes then the world would be a much nicer, not to mention safer, place to live.

I had never experienced racism toward myself until I was in seventh grade. I was starting a new school and didn't know too many people. Kim, my best friend from kindergarten through fifth grade, was going to the same school, and that made me less worried because at least I would already have a ready-made friend. We didn't have one single class together, not even lunch, but we still made an effort to see each other before and after school and between classes, and we talked on the phone. I'm pretty shy, so I hadn't made many friends, but Kim had. I haven't told you yet but Kim is white and so were the friends she made. I quickly became friends with Kim's friends. They were great. They were funny and sweet, but then I would hear the black kids talking: "Yeah, Mia—she always hangs around with those white girls. She must think she's white." They would come up to me and ask me why I hung around with white people—and not even beat around the bush with the question. I mean, what was the big deal?

Then I got called such names as white girl, cracker, and Oreo. I didn't understand why they were making such a big deal out of my having white friends. Not too long after that, I also became friends with this black girl, Ashley, but she was always asking me why I hung around with those white girls instead of with her and her black friends. I usually just shrugged my shoulders and tried not to let the question bother me, since Ashley was my good friend.

Then one day, near the end of the school year, I was talking to Kim and our friends Leslie and Misty when Ashley took me by my arm and told Kim that I was going to hang around with her friends today. So that day I did, and I felt a little out of place. But I felt better because no one was calling me names, and I knew it looked like I fit in. I didn't feel so—I don't know the word—different, I guess.

So I tried to become friends with them, and little by little Kim and I started drifting apart. First I didn't hang around her at school anymore, and we just talked on the phone. But pretty soon I was busy with all my new friends, and all of a sudden, like boom, Kim and I weren't friends anymore. I felt ashamed because all the time she had been such a good friend to me, and all of a sudden I just stopped being there for her and being her friend.

I liked some of my new black friends, but I couldn't act the way I wanted to around them or laugh the way I wanted to around them or even listen to the music I liked around them because it was "being too white." So it was like I had to put on a show when I was around them. And now I'm so used to doing that, I really don't know who I am. But soon I hope to find out.

Another school year has come, and when I walk down the hall and pass Kim I put my head down or pretend to be busy talking to someone and act like I don't see her because I'm full of shame that I would just "betray" her, if that's the word I'm looking for, like that. Sometimes I give a friendly "hi," but then it brings up memories and I feel even worse. If I could go back and change things I would have stayed Kim's friend, but now I feel it's too late to try to be her friend again. If I were her, I wouldn't even want me as a friend.

It still seems that, whatever I do, I can't please the black people because I talk and act "too white" and my skin isn't dark enough.

I think what I learned from this whole experience is that you don't have to try and please anyone but yourself, and you don't have to be anyone but yourself. And don't be afraid to be yourself because it doesn't matter what people think of you, just what you think of yourself.

Linnea Colette Ashley

A self-described military brat, Linnea Colette Ashley was born in California in 1976, but she has lived many places since then. She recently earned a bachelor's degree at Florida A. & M. After a summer internship at the *San Francisco Chronicle*, she hopes to study South African literature in South Africa for a year, and then she wants to teach creative writing to high school students.

In this story, Linnea conveys the anger she feels toward blacks who have judged her by the color of her skin. From fifth grade on, she says, she knew she was never "black enough."

A WASTE OF YELLOW:
GROWING UP BLACK IN AMERICA

Mama never taught me high yella; she was too busy teaching me the differences between black and Negro, darkie and African-American. Who had time for all the shades in between—shades like "swirl" and "sellout" and even that "biracial" name tag that would have been okay if both my parents hadn't been black born and black bred, black loved, and black wed.

Mama sighed, knowing that I would encounter a white world far from friendly sometimes. She had me on the ready, though. She knew it would hurt, but she knew I wouldn't tumble under the weight of ignorance-packed words.

What Mama didn't know, or Daddy either, was that ignorance doesn't see color, and sometimes the word that cuts the deepest isn't a shade of midnight but closer to emerging dawn.

'Cause I was born with gray eyes and a head full of hair that rivaled Diana Ross's and Tina Turner's. And when Mama spit me out I was about as pink as those white babies emerge, enough to make a person question if there had been a mix-up at the hospital.

But no, a few weeks at home and my color filled out to a nice, half-baked yellow-toned brown. So there I was, a potential high-yellow heifer who forgot she was a Negress. What I actually turned out to be was a long-haired, light-eyed, light-skinned tomboy who thought no more of being yellow than I did of being a girl. It was just one of those things that happened to me. I had ovaries (some people told me), and I was lacking some pigment (said some others).

But high yella didn't mean anything more to me than suntan-colored stockings for Sunday morning service and a burning scalp from the relaxer Mama pulled through my longer-than-shoulder-length hair. It was nothing variant from black to me.

Somewhere along the line, I discovered "black power"—and self-hatred. As much as my mother had tried to ready me for the stateside war of the races, she couldn't have prepared me for the soldiers who had been in it so long they became a product of it and lost sight of the true goal.

The first time I remember being ambushed, I was a freshman in high school. I was new to the scene and shy among a school full of strange voices and faces. Even the scent was foreign to me. But what surpassed all else in strangeness was the other students' coldness and the way they avoided me.

People I didn't even know walked close enough to almost jostle me but, instead, jostled me with whispers carefully aimed in my direction:

"High-yella heifer thinks she cute."

"Too good to speak, I guess, with her cat-eyed self."

All I'd done is be new and shy, but I'd managed to commit the greatest offense—I'd been born bright-skinned, light-eyed—and, to top it off, I talked like a white girl.

How dare I?

How dare I be new and anticipate that my own people would embrace what I had always thought was something they could understand—my pigment. They were supposed to be my sistas and brothas. They were supposed to be my family. Instead, they were the source of self-doubt and intimidation.

And it had always been that way. From fifth grade on—that point when we all started discovering whether or not we were colored—I had always been alienated.

I was never black enough. In the seventh grade, when I mingled with the white kids in my "talented" and "gifted" classes and spoke with traces of an Anglo accent, I was the black girl who wasn't black.

Among whites, I was a swirl (their rationalization for me not being a dumb Negro). To blacks, I was an Oreo (their answer to me not fitting a stereotype). And the older I got, the more pronounced the alienation.

Freshman year at my second high school taught me to resent my no-longer-gray but almost hazel eyes. I began to despise the long brown hair and the lighter-than-caramel skin that linked me to the loathsome phrase "high yella."

Sistas spit "high yella" at me when I walked by. Brothas leered at me and oozed "high yella" into a phrase of perversion. And the "blacker-the-berry-the-sweeter-the-juice" people made it an insult.

Again there was the question—how dare I? How dare I not understand that an apology should follow me everywhere—an apology for the massa's blood that was obviously pulsing through my veins, obviously giving me life? How dare I not apologize for having features that mark me as anything except a straight-up-broad-nose-full-lipped-kinky-haired Negro? How dare I not apologize?

I began to question myself. I walked more quickly. I lowered my eyes. I anxiously pulled at my hair. I began to apologize, and I never even realized it.

I'm sorry.

I'm sorry.

I'm sorry that you think I'm beautiful, despite my coloring.

I'm sorry that your boyfriend has been brainwashed to think that high yella can be beautiful at all.

I'm sorry I don't look more like . . .

More like what? That was the question.

I looked just like my father. Who else should I look like? I had hair like my mother's—who else's hair should I have? Daddy's eyes and Mama's lips. Who else's features should I have requested of God before being plopped down on earth?

My insecurities followed me to college. Some at the university regarded me as beautiful. They never saw past my brown eyes, hinting at hazel in the sun, but they regarded me as a beauty anyway. And then there were the other voices, the ones I had become accustomed to hearing:

I wasn't black enough.

I had it easier because America smiled on me and my likeness to whiteness.

Even friends questioned whether or not I shared their plight as a black woman, as if there were a shade of brown that was revered and respected. As if the slightly looser kinks in my hair were noticed and tolerated better than the tight kinks in my darker sistas' hair.

If truth be told, yella was harder on me than black ever was. Not because I received special treatment. Quite the contrary. Yella was harder on me because it robbed me of a haven of acceptance and understanding.

I've always been too dark for white America and too light for black America. Caught in the middle, some strange medium color on a canvas of extremes, I stand out against the rest of the painting, not out of beauty, but out of oddity.

In a world full of extremes, where we're given little boxes in which to classify the American experience, what can I do when I can't fit into them? I'm forced to write my own story and tell the truth as I've experienced it. And how should I begin?

"My name isn't important, just know that I'm a waste of black"? Or, maybe more appropriately, "I'm a waste of yellow"?

Sometimes I have to struggle not to believe that. At those times, I remember that someone once told me I was the color of a Hawaiian sunset. All I could do was smile. It was the nicest way I'd ever heard high yella put.

Caille Millner

***

Now twenty years old and a student at Harvard University, Caille Millner grew up in San Jose, California, where she interned as a writer for the *San Jose Mercury News* when she was a teenager. She had two articles published in the *Washington Post* in 1997 and, since 1995, she has been a writer for Pacific News Service.

"I was lucky enough to receive lessons about the history of American race relations from an early age," she says, noting that white children used to call her nigger and ask her to explain why she looked "that way." Still, she retained her hope in Dr. Martin Luther King Jr.'s dream. "I think that with today's subtle, insidious prejudice, blacks will have to find a different way to achieve Dr. King's dream than the great upheavals of the 1950s and 1960s. But the dream is still worth fighting for."

As she recounts in her story, Caille found herself embroiled in a battle at her high school when she was sixteen years old and had an article published in the *San Jose Mercury News* about racism at her school. Despite the humiliation and the pain of her experience, she says, "I am proud of the way I handled the situation. It helped me learn, among other things, strength and confidence in the power of words." Now she intends to use her gifts as a writer to serve her community and to change the system from the inside.

BLACK CODES: BEHAVIOR IN THE POST–CIVIL RIGHTS ERA

Five hundred and fifty-seven dollars. That's how much it cost me to get my left fender fixed after someone smashed a large object into it. For a fender replacement, the bill wasn't so bad. What hurt more than the bill was the feeling I had when I walked out of school to find the car smashed in what was obviously not an accident.

When I was fourteen, I left an elitist public school with no racial sensitivity and went to an elitist private school with very few people of color. The logic behind this decision was that, while I wouldn't receive much racial support at the new school, at least I would receive a good education. Being one of the only black students was nothing new to me; being one of the only black students who wanted to be black did not come as a surprise either. I had the (mis)fortune of growing up in a tiny black community that strived to distance itself from other black communities as much as possible.

Racism was never overt at my school. It rarely

is anymore—which is one of the travesties of the post–civil rights era. It's difficult to explain to a group of white liberals how the absence of overt hatred does not mean the absence of racism. So when I asked the administration why Black History Month didn't exist at my school, they didn't consider it a deficiency on their part.

"There's really so much else going on right now," they said politely when I asked two years in a row. "But maybe we'll put an announcement in the bulletin."

And when I sat in the back of my freshman world history class, crying because the teacher had said slavery really wasn't that bad, no one thought it constituted a problem.

"It's been hard to integrate blacks into the curriculum of this course," said the teacher. "But I am trying."

As I struggled to maintain a positive sense of identity at school, I was simultaneously forging an idea about my role in the black community. Bourgeois black society wasn't for me, I knew that. Whist and debutante balls didn't fit on my packed agenda of writing, dancing, and thinking. I couldn't meet the gossip requirement, and I wasn't interested primarily in men with the three C's: car, cash, and career.

At the same time, I could never fit into the "other" black community—the "others" on the margins, looking in on society as a whole with hungry eyes. I wasn't streetwise. I had no concept of how to fulfill the complex social requirements for gaining status as a marginalized member of the black community.

I suffered from the isolation of Du Bois's talented tenth. I knew I wanted to serve a community that had no use for me as an individual. There is a psychic peculiarity of being an outsider to an outsiders' group, and I spent most of high school feeling very peculiar.

The summer before my junior year, I met a woman who wanted to know about that psychic peculiarity. Her name was Nell, and she was an editor for Pacific News Service in San Francisco. She was working on a youth newspaper that hired writers from all facets of society: homeless teenagers, skater punks, and high school valedictorians.

I tried to describe what I was going through to her, but I wasn't articulate enough to express my overwhelming alienation from every major group I had ever had contact with. She listened and then told me to pour my emotion out on paper.

I wrote about the racial slights at my school and the difficulty of going to a place where no one understood, or wanted to understand, what it was like to look like me. I wrote about the black community and my struggle for its acceptance. Finally, I wrote about struggling to accept myself and how my real goal for high school was to get a good education and to understand who I really was.

The article took seven or eight major rewrites and a lot of heartache. Some nights I would stay up, exhausted after hours of homework, and cry with frustration over the feelings I couldn't put into words. I did a lot of crying during the writing of that article. It was eventually titled "When Worlds Divide" and was published in a full-page feature in *West*, the Sunday magazine of the *San Jose Mercury News*, on February 11, 1996. I was sixteen years old.

The day the article was published, I read it carefully. My words were there, and for the first time I felt I might have given voice to the emotions I was feeling. But I was also scared. Writing the article had been a catharsis, an act that was bigger than I was and, therefore, out of my control. The fact that it was actually published meant that I would have to suffer the consequences. And from what I knew of progressive white environments, the response would not be kind.

The immediate reaction was a faculty meeting at seven o'clock the following morning to discuss how the school should handle "the situation." The immediate reaction was being called a liar and a slanderer in the halls, being pointed at with anger and hostility. The immediate reaction was what I had steeled myself for. Although I had intended the piece as an article about my identity, the school took it as a personal attack.

The consequences of my article were bigger than either the newspaper or I had expected. West received more letters about my piece than they had received for any single article in months. Most of the public was horrified that I had continued to attend my school. Although I had not named the school, it couldn't have been that hard for readers to figure it out. There weren't many schools like the one I had described in the city of San Jose.

My freshman world history teacher confronted me shortly after the article was published. "You have slandered me and called me a racist," she said. "You don't know what you've done. This is going to affect my career, my family, my entire life."

"I didn't even name you in the article, and I certainly didn't call you a racist," I stammered.

"You took what I said out of context," she said.

"What kind of context can that be put in? You said slavery wasn't that bad. There's no way I can live with that."

The incident with that teacher shook me up, especially when she began talking about me in her classes. I told the principal, who sensed a public-relations disaster and put a stop to her talking about me at once. But that didn't stop her from encouraging one of her students to start a petition against me.

About three days after the article came out, I heard rumors about a petition circulating through the school. I actually managed to get hold of the document for a few minutes. It was a petition to "support" the school administration; it also called for disciplinary action against me.

What surprised me the most about the petition was the number of people who had signed it. At least seventy-five students—the majority of the senior class—had signed the petition over the course of the two days it had been circulating. These were people I knew, people I had been friendly with, even some I had grown up with. I found out later that very few of them had actually read the article, much less thought about what I had said.

The next week an unsigned threat arrived in the mail. "You had better watch out, driving that big yellow car with your name on the license plates," the letter taunted. (I drove a "character car," a 1983 mustard-yellow Volvo.) I gave the letter to my mother for posterity and didn't think much about it.

Then I walked out of school a few days later and found my car smashed.

After the petition came out, I wasn't sure I could make it. I was frightened by the amount of hatred my words had stirred up. I was also afraid. Would the administration take action against me, as they had intimated they might? I was also sick of being hated by all the students. I didn't regret publishing my article by any means, but I didn't know if I could last another year and a half at my school.

Fortunately, I got angry. The destruction of my car stirred me to act. I came to the conclusion that if I was going to be a pariah, I would at least teach the school who they were dealing with. My friend from Pacific News Service, Nell, and my mother went to talk to the principal and warn him that any "disciplinary" action against me would result in a swift lawsuit. We alerted the local branch of the NAACP, who immediately assured us that they would support us. The editor at *West* also pledged her support. Sure enough, the hostility died down. No more threats. No more petitions.

I kept writing, which was my response to the threats. I was extremely prolific for the next year and a half, publishing in newspapers around the country. The greatest irony is that the administration wound up loving me when I became the first student ever from my school to get into Harvard University, where I'm now finishing my first year.

Selected Chronology

1863   The Emancipation Proclamation is signed by President Abraham Lincoln, freeing the slaves in the Confederacy during the Civil War.

1865   The Civil War ends. Congress passes the Thirteenth Amendment to the Constitution, abolishing slavery in the entire U.S. Nearly 4 million slaves are declared free.

1868   The Fourteenth Amendment to the Constitution is passed, declaring that all people born in the United States are citizens and guaranteeing all citizens equal protection under the law.

1870   The Fifteenth Amendment to the Constitution is passed, guaranteeing the right to vote to all citizens, regardless of race. (Note: Although the Fifteenth Amendment grants rights to adult black males, women are still not allowed to vote. The right to vote in federal elections is not granted in all states until the Nineteenth Amendment, in 1920.)

    In spite of the ratification of the Thirteenth, Fourteenth, and Fifteenth amendments, Southern states enact laws that enforce racial separation. These laws come to be known as Jim Crow laws, named after a song made popular in minstrel shows (in which whites performed in blackface). Black and white people may not legally engage in activities such as eating together in a public place, worshipping together, riding on a train or bus together, or even drinking from the same water fountain.

1896   In the case of *Plessy v. Ferguson*, the U.S. Supreme Court upholds Louisiana's 1890 Separate Car Law, which declared that accommodations can be racially segregated so long as those for blacks are equal to those for whites. In 1896 a group of concerned black citizens test the law by having Homer Adolph Plessy, a black man, sit in the "whites only" car on a passenger train and refuse to move to the "colored" car. This "separate but equal" doctrine of racial segregation remains until 1954, when the Supreme Court begins to overturn these state laws as unconstitutional.

1909   The NAACP (National Association for the Advancement of Colored People) is founded in New York City on February 12, the centennial of Abraham Lincoln's birth. Over the decades the organization, through nonviolent means, fights for the political, educational, social, and economic equality of all minorities.

1910   The National Urban League is founded to open
        up job opportunities for black people.

1925   Black Pullman Car workers, working under
        extreme conditions for low pay, form the
        Brotherhood of Sleeping Car Porters in New
        York City. Labor leader A. Philip Randolph is
        elected the union's first president. In 1935 the
        union becomes the first black union to be affili-
        ated with the American Federation of Labor
        (AFL).

1929   January 15—Martin Luther King Jr. is born.

1938   In the case of *Missouri ex rel. Gaines v. Canada*,
        the U.S. Supreme Court rules that black stu-
        dents in each state must be given educational
        facilities equal to those of whites, reinforcing
        the 1896 separate-but-equal doctrine.

1942   After a campaign protesting discrimination in
        a Chicago restaurant, the Congress of Racial
        Equality (CORE) is founded by James Farmer.

1954   In the case of *Brown v. Board of Education of
        Topeka*, the U.S. Supreme Court reverses *Plessy
        v. Ferguson* and bans segregation in public
        schools.

1955   Rosa Parks refuses to give up her seat to
        a white person on a public bus in Montgomery,
        Alabama, and is arrested. This action leads
        to a black boycott of buses by the Montgomery
        Improvement Association that lasts more than

a year. Dr. Martin Luther King Jr.'s leadership of the boycott brings about his national prominence.

1956   Martin Luther King Jr.'s home in Montgomery, Alabama, is bombed.

The Montgomery bus boycott is successful, and city buses are desegregated.

1957   A group of black ministers meets at Dr. Martin Luther King Sr.'s church, the Ebenezer Baptist Church, in Atlanta, Georgia, to coordinate the efforts of civil rights groups. The result is the formation of the Southern Christian Leadership Conference (SCLC), with Martin Luther King Jr. as its president.

The Civil Rights Act of 1957 is signed by President Dwight D. Eisenhower, establishing a civil rights commission within the Justice Department and giving the federal government the authority to act in support of the Supreme Court's ban on school segregation.

When Governor Orval Faubus calls in the Arkansas National Guard to prohibit students from desegregating the all-white Central High School in Little Rock, President Eisenhower federalizes the National Guard and sends in federal troops to restore order and to escort nine black students into Central High School.

1960   Students in Greensboro, North Carolina, arrange sit-ins at all-white lunch counters to push for desegregation in public places. Sit-ins and other nonviolent demonstrations follow in many Southern towns and cities and across the nation.

The Student Nonviolent Coordinating Committee (SNCC) is formed in Raleigh, North Carolina, by black and white college students seeking to speed desegregation in the South. Founding members include Julian Bond, H. Rap Brown, Stokely Carmichael, and John Lewis.

1961   Freedom Riders, both black and white, board a bus in Washington, D.C., heading for New Orleans. Their plan is to ride through the South to make sure that the Supreme Court decision declaring unconstitutional the segregation of public areas for interstate travelers—waiting rooms, rest rooms, and restaurants—is complied with. More Freedom Rides take place through the summer.

1962   Desegregation reaches college campuses as James Meredith becomes the first black student to enroll in the University of Mississippi. Two students are killed in the rioting that breaks out on campus to protest his presence.

1963   In Birmingham, Alabama, Dr. King and other ministers are arrested during a peaceful demonstration (a "kneel-in") to protest the segregation of churches. Angry crowds protest the arrest, and the police respond with dogs and fire hoses.

Medgar Evers, leader of the Mississippi chapter of the NAACP, is assassinated.

Two hundred fifty thousand people attend the March on Washington to show their support for pending civil rights legislation. Dr. King delivers his "I Have a Dream" speech at the Lincoln Memorial.

Four black girls are killed by a bomb in the basement of a church in Birmingham, Alabama.

1964   The Civil Rights Act, guaranteeing equal access to public places and outlawing discrimination in the workplace, is passed by Congress and signed into law by President Lyndon B. Johnson.

Dr. Martin Luther King Jr. receives the Nobel Peace Prize.

Civil rights workers James Chaney, Andrew Goodman, and Michael Schwerner, who are among 800 volunteers helping people register to vote, are murdered near the town of Philadelphia, Mississippi. The deputy sheriff of Philadelphia and six others are convicted of the crime. All are members of the Ku Klux Klan, a white supremacist secret vigilante group founded in 1866.

1965   Black Muslim leader Malcolm X is assassinated in New York City.

To protest the killing of a demonstrator by a state trooper in Marion, Alabama, Martin Luther King Jr. attempts to lead a peaceful march from Selma, Alabama, to Montgomery, the state capital, to appeal to Governor George Wallace to stop police brutality and to call attention to the struggle for voters' rights. When Governor Wallace bans the march, Dr. King goes to Washington to speak with President Johnson. Six hundred marchers proceed despite the ban and are beaten by state troopers. This day becomes known as Bloody Sunday.

With the protection of federal troops, Dr. King leads the fifty-two-mile march from Selma to Montgomery. A white civil rights worker, Viola Liuzzo, is killed as she transports some of the marchers back to their homes.

The Voting Rights Act of 1965 bans illegal state literacy voter qualification tests and opens the door for black voter registration by federal registrars if states refuse to comply.

Riots erupt in the Watts section of Los Angeles to protest the arrest of a young black driver on suspicion of drunk driving by the highway patrol. More than thirty people are killed in the riots.

1966   The Black Panther party is founded by Huey P. Newton and Bobby Seale in Oakland, California, in response to police brutality in Watts and other urban areas. This new political party issues a ten-point program of self-determination for the black community, focusing on equal employment, housing, and social programs to fight poverty.

The new chairman of SNCC, Stokely Carmichael, calls for "black power."

1967   Thurgood Marshall, a lawyer for the NAACP
        Legal Defense and Education Fund, is con-
        firmed as the first black U.S. Supreme Court
        justice.

        Stokely Carmichael leaves SNCC to join the
        Black Panthers.

1968   Shirley Chisholm of New York is elected to the
        U.S. House of Representatives, the first black
        woman to be elected to Congress.

        Martin Luther King Jr. leads a march for
        striking sanitation workers in Memphis,
        Tennessee. Dr. King announces his plans for a
        Poor People's Campaign.

        April 3—Dr. King gives his last speech,
        "I See the Promised Land" (also known as
        "I've Been to the Mountaintop"), in Memphis,
        Tennessee.

        April 4—Dr. Martin Luther King Jr. is assas-
        sinated in Memphis, Tennessee. In response to
        the assassination, riots erupt nationwide.

        The Poor People's Campaign goes on with-
        out Dr. King. More than 50,000 people march
        on Washington, D.C.

        The Civil Rights Act, also known as the Fair
        Housing Act, makes it illegal to discriminate
        on the basis of race, color, religion, or national
        origin in the rental or sale of housing.

1971   The Supreme Court rules that busing for the
        purpose of achieving school desegregation is
        constitutional.

        Reverend Jesse Jackson is a moving force
        behind the founding of Operation PUSH

(People United to Save Humanity), an international human rights organization dedicated to education and economic equality.

1979   Members of the Ku Klux Klan shoot and kill five people at an anti–Ku Klux Klan rally in Greensboro, North Carolina, once again calling national attention to the Klan's activities.

1988   Reverend Jesse Jackson runs for President of the United States.

1989   Army General Colin L. Powell becomes the first black chairman of the Joint Chiefs of Staff of the U.S. Armed Forces.

     Douglas Wilder of Virginia becomes the first black state governor.

1992   Carol Moseley Braun of Illinois becomes the first black woman to be elected to the U.S. Senate.

     Riots erupt in South Central Los Angeles after a jury acquits four white police officers of criminal charges in the beating of Rodney King, a black motorist. The incident had been caught on videotape.

1993   Two of the four police officers acquitted of assault charges for Rodney King's beating are found guilty of violating his civil rights.

1997   Two white men are charged with murder for burning and beheading Garnett P. Johnson, a black man, in Independence, Virginia. The murder is designated a racially motivated hate crime.

1998   In Jasper, Texas, three white supremacists associated with the Ku Klux Klan beat James Byrd Jr., a disabled black man, and drag him to his death behind a pickup truck.

1999   John William King, one of the three men accused of killing James Byrd Jr., is found guilty and receives the death penalty. In a separate trial, another of the men, Lawrence Russell Brewer, is found guilty and also receives the death penalty. In another trial, Shawn Allen Berry, the third man, is found guilty and sentenced to life in prison.

Credits

———◆———

"A Waste of Yellow: Growing Up Black in America," ©
Linnea Colette Ashley, Houston, Texas, 1999.

"Boomerism, or Doing Time in the Ivy League," © Ben
Bates, Guthrie, Oklahoma, 1999.

"My First Friend (My Blond-Haired, Blue-Eyed
Linda)," © Marion Coleman Brown, Zachary,
Louisiana, 1999.

"Silver Stars," © J. K. Dennis, Carbondale, Illinois, 1999.

"The Lesson" by Dianne E. Dixon was previously published in a different form in *Shooting Star Review* (©
October 1995). It is published here by permission of
the author.

"Fred," © LeVan D. Hawkins, West Hollywood,
California, 1999.

"Sticks and Stones and Words and Bones," © Amitiyah
Elayne Hyman, Washington, D.C., 1999.

"Hitting Dante," © Aya de León, Berkeley, California,
1999.

"Black Codes: Behavior in the Post–Civil Rights Era," ©
Caille Millner, Cambridge, Massachusetts, 1999.

"Child of the Dream," © Charisse Nesbit, Newark,
Delaware, 1999.

"All the Black Children," © Antoine P. Reddick,
Somers, Connecticut, 1999.

About the Author

Laurel Holliday, formerly a college teacher, editor, and psychotherapist, now writes full time in Seattle. She is the award-winning author of the Children of Conflict series: *Children in the Holocaust and World War II: Their Secret Diaries; Children of "The Troubles": Our Lives in the Crossfire of Northern Ireland;* and *Children of Israel, Children of Palestine: Our Own True Stories.* Those three volumes were collected and abridged in the Archway Paperback edition titled *Why Do They Hate Me?: Young Lives Caught in War and Conflict. Dreaming in Color, Living in Black and White* is an abridged edition of Holliday's fourth title in the Children of Conflict series, *Children of the Dream: Our Own Stories of Growing Up Black in America.* Laurel Holliday is also the author of *Heartsongs*, an international collection of young girls' diaries, which won a Best Book for Young Adults Award from the American Library Association.